THE QUESTI
DISABILITY,

Policies towards 'access' and 'inclusion' are politically mandated and largely unquestioned in contemporary educational institutions. But many methods of addressing accessibility – installing signs, ramps, and accessible washrooms – essentially frame disability as a problem to be 'fixed.' *The Question of Access* investigates the social meanings of access on university campuses from the perspective of cultural disability studies.

Through narratives of struggle and analyses of policy and everyday practices, Tanya Titchkosky shows how interpretations of access reproduce problematic conceptions not only of who belongs, but also when and where. Titchkosky examines how the bureaucratization of access issues has affected understandings of our lives together in social space. Using the idea of access as a starting point as to how disability can be rethought, *The Question of Access* challenges readers to question critically their own perceptions of disability and access.

TANYA TITCHKOSKY is an associate professor and an associate department chair at the Ontario Institute for Studies in Education, University of Toronto.

TANYA TITCHKOSKY

The Question of Access

Disability, Space, Meaning

UNIVERSITY OF TORONTO PRESS
Toronto Buffalo London

© University of Toronto Press 2011
Toronto   Buffalo   London
www.utppublishing.com
Printed in Canada

ISBN 978-1-4426-4026-9 (cloth)
ISBN 978-1-4426-1000-2 (paper)

Printed on acid-free, 100% post-consumer recycled paper with vegetable-based inks.

Library and Archives Canada Cataloguing in Publication

Titchkosky, Tanya, 1966–
The question of access : disability, space, meaning/Tanya Titchkosky.

Includes bibliographical references and index.
ISBN 978-1-4426-4026-9 (bound).   ISBN 978-1-4426-1000-2 (pbk.)

1. People with disabilities – Education (Higher) – Ontario – Toronto.
2. People with disabilities – Ontario – Toronto – Social conditions.
3. College students with disabilities – Ontario – Toronto – Social conditions.
4. Social integration – Ontario – Toronto.   5. Sociology of disability.   I. Title.

LC4814.C32T58 2011   371.9'047409713541   C2011-902656-2

University of Toronto Press acknowledges the financial assistance to its publishing program of the Canada Council for the Arts and the Ontario Arts Council.

Canada Council   Conseil des Arts
for the Arts   du Canada

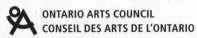

ONTARIO ARTS COUNCIL
CONSEIL DES ARTS DE L'ONTARIO

University of Toronto Press acknowledges the financial support of the Government of Canada through the Canada Book Fund for its publishing activities.

To Rod

The truth about stories is that that's all we are.

Thomas King, *The Truth about Stories*

Disability studies must recognize that its critique should be trained on the institution of the academy as much as on the social and political context outside its walls.

Sharon Snyder and David Mitchell,
Cultural Locations of Disability

You know, I mean, things just weren't built with people with disabilities in mind. That's why there are no accessible washrooms here.

Anonymous

To understand being is to exist in such a way that one takes care of one's own existence. To understand is to take care. Exactly how does this understanding, this solicitude come about? The phenomenon of the world, or more precisely, the structure of 'being-in-the-world' presents the precise form in which this understanding of being is realized.

Emmanuel Levinas, 'Martin Heidegger and Ontology'

Contents

Preface

This book explores the social meaning of access from a disability studies perspective. The University of Toronto is the site of this exploration. *The Question of Access* presents a unique critical analysis of an undertheorized topic, namely, what do contemporary access issues regarding disability in bureaucratic systems, such as the academy, actually *do* to our understanding of our lives together in social space?

Common expressions about access and inclusion buzz around many university environments as unquestioned values. As Roger Slee (2008: 104) reminds us, the repetitive vocabulary of inclusion 'deployed to saturation levels' dulls imagination and imperils the possibility of real change. But we can wonder about what is really meant when people talk about access, struggle for inclusion, or even get surprised when issues of access arise. This book is dedicated to understanding access as a complex form of perception that organizes socio-political relations between people in social space – in this case, the space of a large and diverse urban university in Canada. Processes of inclusion, and thus access, can arise only insofar as exclusion has already become an issue and is already perceivable. All endeavours to address access issues and disability contain within them not only efficacious plans and programs, but also questions – questions that we need to explicitly ask and whose meaning is yet unclear. By studying what has already been said and done on behalf of access, we can begin to wonder about access, understand it, and perhaps even approach it differently.

While access and inclusion often seem like unquestioned values, it is also true that some people have to fight for access while others are shocked or even irritated by this fight. How access is regarded has much to do with how disability does and does not appear in the situations in which we find ourselves. *The Question of Access* marks a moment where we can begin to wonder about the presence and absence of disability in the academy and this means addressing how some people have unquestioned access to social space while others do not. After all, the academy is part of a neo-liberal context where it is generally assumed that 'we all' value access and desire inclusion.

In the following pages I explore how the value of access is spoken of, acted upon, and sometimes resisted in university life. This exploration is oriented to revealing the complicated character of our lives together as bodied beings in social space. I aim to demonstrate that the relation between bodies and social space is much more ambiguous than it first appears. How we actually come to live together in the spaces where we do is built from yet-to-be examined conceptions of who disabled people[1] are; of what disability means; of when access can and cannot appear as an important issue; and of where access can be questioned and where it cannot. For my purposes, access is a questioning orientation, an important way to perceive, speak of, and take action on the relations between bodies and social space.

The aim of this book is to be guided by a politics of wonder and thus to think through the relationship between access and disability, and our lives together, in new ways. By politics of wonder I mean pausing in the face of what already *is*. Pausing allows us to face what is already said and done in the name of access, not in order to evaluate efficacy, but instead to uncover the sensibility and the meaning that lie there. What has already been said or done in the name of access is an occasion for questions oriented to discerning the meaning of our interrelations in social space. Proceeding with such theorizing is political in that it necessarily remakes the assumed clarity of what is already done and said into a place of questions where doubt can open on to new horizons of possibility.

The issues of the place of access are both more and less than we might first think. In 1982, disability was included in the Canadian Charter of Rights and Freedoms and thus became a prohibited ground of exclusion. And yet, while it is neither legal nor decent to bar disabled people from participation – to, for example, block people from attending classes, events, or visiting offices, using technology, and so on – such barriers and exclusions are still real in university life. This reality is reflected in the following fact: Faculty and staff who identify as having a disability at the University of Toronto, one of Canada's largest universities, comprise less than 3 per cent of the entire employee population; a population that should reflect a disability rate of more than 15 per cent

(U of T, 2008: 7). While disability is not a justifiable reason to exclude people from participation in the realms subject to the Charter, simply including 'mental or physical disability' in the categories of non-discrimination has certainly not meant the end of discrimination for anyone. There are a multitude of ways that wide gaps can open between people and their rights and the possibility of legitimate participation.

Beginning with the understanding that exclusion on the basis of disability is still a routine practice, what has captured my attention most of all – and has given rise to a profound sense of disquiet – are the myriad ways that the everyday practices of exclusion and inclusion are not noticed and thus made to disappear. I am most interested in examining how the lack of access for disabled people (and thus our absence) is naturalized to such an extent that even when barriers and processes of exclusion are noticed they are still conceived as somehow natural, reasonable, sensible, and even seemingly justifiable. Further, it seems that some bureaucratic mechanisms of inclusion might actually serve to normalize the ongoing exclusion of disabled people. The ways in which people make it seem normal to dis-attend to the presence and absence of disability is what has prodded my imagination in these pages.

Let me give one example. At the University of Toronto, disability is simply left out of the faculty's non-discrimination clause found in its governing documents. In the legally binding document that sets out the basic employee relations between faculty, librarians, and the University administration, this omission appears in this way:

Article 9: No Discrimination

The parties agree that there shall be no discrimination, interference, restriction, or coercion exercised or practiced toward any faculty member or librarian in respect to salaries, fringe benefits, pensions, rank, promotion, tenure, reappointment, dismissal, research or other leaves, or any other terms and conditions of employment by reason of age (except for retirement as provided for in this Agreement), race, creed, colour, national origin, citizenship, religious or political affiliation or belief, sex, sexual orientation, marital status and/or family relationship, place of residence, membership or activity in the Association, or any activity pursuant to the principles of academic freedom set out in Article 5. (University of Toronto, n.d.)

Where is disability on this list? In 2006, when I brought this to the attention of faculty, the faculty association, and a vice president, there was noticeable shock and then silence. Despite bringing this exclusion of disability to people's attention, the absence of disability remains un-addressed. In 2010, for example, while serving on a committee for the selection of a departmental chair as well as on a faculty hiring commit-tee, we were reminded of the 'no discrimination' clause as this was to inform the selection process. Again, the mention of disability was made when it was pointed out that it was missing from both the literature and the discussion. Once more, there was shock and then silence. It is this paradoxical social reality of disability's presence yet absence, of its partial inclusion, or what I have theorized elsewhere as 'disability's in-clusion as an excludable type,' that I am captivated by and seek to more fully understand throughout *The Question of Access*.

The ambiguous positioning of disability in the university today is, most likely, not due solely to blatant hate, straightforward ignorance, or inadequate procedures, nor is the University of Toronto a unique case in point. After all, it is 'we,' both we who do and we who do not address disability and access issues, who constitute disability as an under-theorized phenomenon that has remained relatively untouched by any collective need for further analysis. This *we* is located where conceptions of disability and bureaucratic forms of participation inter-sect. This is why we should be interested in examining the ambiguous positioning of disability as both in/out; included/excluded; and partial participant, as these are achieved, and re-achieved, through ordinary daily interactions in university life. I show how these unexamined con-ceptions of disability inform new policy and practice and serve to help reproduce disability as it is already constituted. So, I am not pointing to a single university as a unique perpetrator of discrimination, nor am I interested in fixing blame to a person, a procedure, or an office. On the contrary, this analysis resists any form of individualizing of disability.

Universities in general often claim a commitment to a multicultural and an equity agenda and express an interest in leading communities, and even nations, to implement social change that embraces diversity. It would seem obvious, for example, that discussions of access should involve a diversity of people and a multicultural awareness and thus invite a complex array of disability issues. Moreover, discussions of access should include more than the obvious exclusion of wheelchair users and individualized accommodation processes for those with learning differences. It should be reasonable to assume that discus-sions of disability and access will include a consideration of all sorts of embodiments, health issues, or ethnic, religious, or sexuality com-mitments, and these interlock with issues of race, class, and gender. All of this is easy enough to imagine. However, the academy is not yet a place where diversity is located *in* disability or where the difference of disability is welcomed and imagined in diverse ways. The university does, however, discuss those with disabilities as 'problem students' and asks what to do with them, thus reproducing disability as an individual problem.

That the question of access is ordinarily raised in bureaucratic orders of daily life in regular, non-diverse, and non-imaginative ways is my starting point. I also pursue the idea that the most ordinary or acceptable ways to speak of access and its improvement may in fact be a major barrier to the improvement of access. I attend to ordinary practices in one locale since an intense focus on the ordinary things said and done on behalf of the questions of access can reveal the actual conceptions of disability at work in access fights, policy, and discussions. I also do not survey the depth of the problem of disability exclusions even though this might provide a more vivid sense of the extent of the problem. My aim is only to show how the problem of inclusion and exclusion actually works at the everyday level of bureaucratized life by the use of unexamined conceptions of bodies and social space. Such an aim is not served well by surveys.

This book, then, closely attends what we are actually doing and saying in relation to disability and access, and does not attend to idealized plans for better access in the future. Attending to what otherwise remains a taken-for-granted operation in university life is the beginning of cultivating a new, expanded version of disability that could be more connected to other forms of difference. Disability and questions of access can thus be represented in far more diverse ways by awaking a desire for them to be something other than the same.

Acknowledgments

There are many people to thank. For financial support I thank the Social Sciences and Humanities Research Council of Canada for a Standard SSHRC Grant entitled 'Organizing Disablement: The University and Disability Experience,' with co-investigator Rod Michalko. I am also grateful to the University of Toronto for the Connaught New Faculty Start-Up Grant; as well as to the Ontario Institute for Studies in Education of the University of Toronto (OISE/UT) for providing research assistance and financial support, especially Associate Dean Normand Labrie. Once again, thank you Virgil Duff (now retired), Executive Acquisition Editor, for all that you have done for so many authors. For supportive music and musings, I thank the Loyal Clams, the Bill Norman Trio, and The Big Fog. There is a large and dynamic group of graduate students at OISE/UT to whom I owe a debt of thanks. It has been especially invigorating working together on questions of access as both a space of theorizing and political action. In particular, I thank Eliza Chandler and Anne McGuire, as well as Liwliwa Tores, Ji-Eun Lee, Somani Ferley, and Sarah Snyder, for the special touch they have added to this book through their readings, conversations, and/or research assistance. I am grateful to the faculty and staff in my Department of Sociology and Equity Studies in Education at OISE/UT who continue to demonstrate a collective sense that critical theoretical engagement can make a difference in how we relate to and live in the world. In particular, I have been touched by conversations with Kari Dehli, Sherene Razack, and Rinaldo Walcott, especially for their provocations regarding the meaning of human. I am indebted to Cheryl Williams for the enjoyment she has taken in this project and the other staff members who provided many stories of how access and disability need to be considered anew. The scholars and artists in the Society for Disability Studies have provided an example of how questioning access can be a communal practice and also a space to theorize for which I am deeply grateful. I have been influenced by innumerable disabled people who have been teaching me that desiring to live in community with disability can happen in lively and unexpected ways. Finally, and again, I thank Rod Michalko, who is part of all of the relations mentioned above but also my partner in love, learning, and life and so is conversant with all that is within these pages. With Rod translating my dyslexic expressions into a far more readable text, this book came to fruition. I owe a special thanks to you, Rod.

THE QUESTION OF ACCESS:
DISABILITY, SPACE, MEANING

1 Introduction: Access as an Act of Perception

Embodied Interpretation

Access – it sometimes seems as though some people have it and some don't. But what if access is much more than such an individual state of affairs? What if access is much more than a substantial, measurable entity? What if it is more like a way of judging or a way of perceiving?

Some of the time people orient to self, others, spaces, and events as issues of access.[1] Sometimes access comes up as a question, at other times as an answer, and at still other times it doesn't come up at all. Nonetheless, taken-for-granted conceptions of who has an access issue, and what access means, influence how people perceive these issues and act upon them. This means that 'access' *is* a way of bringing life to consciousness, a form of oriented social action, and a way of relating to people and places (Weber, 1947: 88). Access, in this sense, is an interpretive relation between bodies. In this conception, we can explore how people wonder about and act within social space – and discover how we are enmeshed in the activity of making people and places meaningful to one another.

Given that questions of access can arise for anyone, at any time, and anywhere for innumerable reasons, access is a way people have of relating to the ways they are embodied as beings in the particular places where they find themselves. By 'embodied' I mean all the ways we have to sense, feel, and move in the world, as these are mediated by the interests of social environments, including race, class, gender, and sexual orientation. Access is a way to orient to, and even come to wonder about, who, what, where, and when we find ourselves to be in social space. Through the perceptual consciousness of 'access,' people take social life into account as a space of questions regarding who belongs where, under what auspices or qualifications, and during what times or through what particular thresholds. Access, then, is tied to the social organization of participation, even to belonging. Access not only needs to be sought out and fought for, legally secured, physically measured, and politically protected, it also needs to be understood – as a complex form of perception that organizes socio-political relations between people in social space. My place of work, the University of Toronto, is the particular space from which my analysis proceeds – I study the way access is and is not spoken about and acted upon in the educational setting of this large, urban university in Canada.

Now, what if, like access, we treat disability as a way of perceiving and orienting to the world rather than conceiving of it as an individual functional limitation? While we all have bodies – bodies that we act, sense, feel, or move in and through – only some bodies, only some of the time and only in some places, are understood as disabled ones. There are a number of ways of conceiving of disability but my aim is not to point out the plethora of embodied differences, nor do I want to develop an exhaustive enumeration of the barriers faced by disabled people. Instead, I wish to question how we do and don't pay attention to disability. This means that disability is a way of perceiving, a form of interpretation, a way to orient not only to people, but also to places, things, and events – especially if we understand these people, places, things, and events as unfortunate. This close tie to misfortune (Shklar, 1990) occurs, in part, because 'disability' is a term that typically animates forms of everyday perception shaped by a taken-for-granted able-ism. Through able-ism, a conception of disability informed by the primacy of normalcy, people perceive that the streetcar is disabled; traffic flow is crippled; the last bad call of the umpire proves he is blind; the president was deaf to the suffering of the people after the disaster, offering only lame excuses which paralysed communities; your antics are so retarded, just crazy, you are driving us insane, in fact, the times are insane, such an anxious day with the economy amputated by recession, people are failing to sit still and read the stand-up work being done by some to trim their excess fat and show that they have a backbone and can step up to the plate. Come on, stand up for your rights! And we can also say, perhaps in an equally able-ist way, 'I am sorry, have you always been disabled?' From more politically aware positions, it is also common to say that being a woman under patriarchy is to face disablement; being racialized in settler societies is to face disablement; and that most forms of exclusion, marginalization, or devaluation entail disablement. These are some of the myriad ways, always interconnected to issues of race, class, and gender, that people perceive the category of disability.

Almost any undesirable state of affairs, even a slight difference from the norm, is today depicted through the language of disability. This language grants us access to conceptions of disability since we notice devalued differences in and through these concepts. It is through conceptions of disability that places, things, and events are perceived and relations to them organized, even governed (Foucault, 1988, 1980). This means that disability is a prominent 'sense-making' device, a kind of language used to make sense of all that which troubles us in contemporary times.

And there is more. Disability is a concept that gives access, not only to calamities, world events, and undesirable states of affairs, but also to people. The disabled, people with disabilities, disabled individuals – these terms, too, represent concepts used to notice and orient self and other.[2] Whether as self-identification or as a label for groups or individuals, disability is also a way to perceive and make sense of the bodies, minds, senses, emotions, comportments, and even gestures of people.

When used to relate to people, disability is a form of perception that typically devalues an embodied difference. Some noticeable departure from the desired and expected is often taken as disability. To conceive of something as disability can be understood as an oriented act of perception, intimately tied to evaluation that guides interaction. This orientation grounds the critical understanding that disability should be regarded as that which exists between people; one cannot be disabled alone (Dossa, 2009, 2006; Michalko, 2002; Parekh, 2006; Snyder and Mitchell, 2006a, 2006b; Titchkosky, 2007a, 2003a). The World Health Organization (WHO, 1980), in contrast, holds that disability is a 'loss or abnormality' in people's bodies, minds, or senses which prevents people from participating in ways 'considered normal for a human being,' and this is a shared global orientation today. This dominant interpretation takes for granted the devaluation of disability and tacitly relies on the concept of non-disability as normal and disability as a negative, abnormal condition with which some people must deal.

Individualized conceptions of disability, such as the WHO's, require that impairment be treated *as if* it is the cause of disabled peoples' lack of participation in education, employment, leisure, and love. A further issue with individualizing disability is that this perception can act as a barrier to reflection on who and what is considered disabled. It can also prevent us from noticing when and where we use the concept of disability – not to mention how we use it. The lack of a need for reflection on how we perceive disability can squelch the desire to wonder about the meaning of the concept within our ways of knowing and governing self and other under contemporary conditions. And this has consequences.

Disability is a key way of constitutively perceiving non-normalcy; it is a way of referring to and dealing with that which is regarded as anomalous and is almost always devalued. This means that the concept of disability gives us access to certain people, places, and events, but it does so while shoring up a belief in a naturalized version of access: one either has access or does not; one personally needs access or does not. Through unexamined relations to both disability and non-disability, the idea that the world is 'naturally' for some and not for others is reproduced. A failure to attend to the ways the world is naturalized, and thus to appear 'naturally' there only for some, is the basic premise of the social processes of able-ism, patriarchy, and colonialism. (For a critique of the process of naturalization, consider Césaire, 1972; Farley, 1997; Michalko, 2002, 1999; Razack, 2010, 2008.) It seems 'only natural' that some forms of embodied existence have trouble accessing the stuff of daily life, such as it is. But this act of naturalizing some bodies as naturally lacking access and, therefore, excludable provides immediate, unquestioned access to daily life *as if* it too is natural.

But it is possible to nurture a desire to wonder about the everyday act of perceiving disability. This wondering is focused on questioning the relations between disability, space, and access. Through an emphasis on disability, this book participates in the project of denaturalizing what seems to be 'natural' exclusion, a project it shares with inquiries such as critical race studies, queer studies, and various feminisms. Exploring the meanings of access is, fundamentally, the exploration of the meaning of our lives together – who is together with whom, how, where, when, and why? Once we recognize this, we can begin to regard disability as a valuable interpretive space for denaturalizing our existence and complicating singular or totalizing ways of making meaning as bodied beings. Denaturalizing existence does not require us to deny the materiality of the body, nor that of social space, but it certainly does make the relation *between* people and places a significant, historical, material fact, worthy of concerted critical reflection.

People and Places

Between the issue of access and the perception of disability lies an over-flow of questions. As a way to enter this space of questions, I proceed with a consideration of my experiences of access issues during the first few years of my work as a professor at the Ontario Institute for Studies in Education at the University of Toronto (OISE/UT). My disability studies position in the department of Sociology and Equity Studies in Education at OISE/UT in 2006 immediately hooked me into a host of access issues. These issues first took shape as a plethora of concerns about missing resources in the university environment that shook my sense of legitimacy. There were no accessible washrooms and few electronic door openers; there were few faculty or student offices that could admit a wheelchair user; there were no parking spaces, no mailboxes, no photocopying machines, no library spaces, and no computers easily accessible to disabled people. What place could disability studies have in a location that sported little space for disabled people? How could I continue to collect a pay cheque and develop disability studies in a workplace where able-bodied-based privilege was necessary for participation?

As obvious as it is that the physical environment is materially organized so as to make participation difficult, if not impossible, for some people, it is not obvious how this exclusion sustains itself. Yet some people have access to university life while others do not; this discrepancy is not merely a fight between the haves and the have-nots, nor only an argument of who is in and who out. The appearance of such a discrepancy is not obvious and straightforward, but it is a complicated socio-political phenomenon. Moreover, it is not clear where, when, or why things change and access becomes a critical feature of a collective's perception of a place.

Despite its complicated meaning, access seems to enter our lives not so much as a question but as a demand. In the university, for example, people require access to buildings, washrooms, classrooms, offices, or access to filling out forms; people require access to news, policies, and reading lists, as well as to professors and events; people require access to a sense of the camaraderie, conversation, and connections that accompany academic life. In short, people require access to a general feeling of legitimate participation, meaningfulness, and belonging. A classroom, a policy, or a professor can be perceived through questions of access.

Such a perception can give rise to a variety of judgments including that rights are being violated, that participation is being barred, that this is 'just the way things are,' or that the question of access is beneath notice since it does not appear as a real concern.

Even though access issues have been addressed by legislative procedures, particularly in the UK and U.S., access in even these countries remains something to analyse since it represents the question of legitimacy of social space for all. The point, though, is not to document access legislation around the world and call out their differences. Developing legislative procedures for inclusion and non-discrimination means, after all, that access is a struggle and uncertain. I proceed from the understanding that all endeavours to address access issues contain within them not only legislation, plans, and programs, but also questions – questions that we all need to know we are asking and questions whose meaning for contemporary society is yet to be ascertained. Such questioning brings to consciousness the complicated matter of meaning-making that always arises between people and places, between bodies and social space.

All of these potential shifts in the perception of access have led me to regard the straightforward denial of access, as well as explicit demands for more access, as interpretive scenes. Within these scenes, we can explore established relations between bodies and social space. What interests me most are the relationships between people and places that are recognized as 'bureaucratic' in character since, within the contemporary university system, access and inclusion issues are almost always addressed through bureaucratic processes.

Bureaucracy

'Bureaucracy' refers to a hierarchal and regularized form of structured procedure usually managed by an office or official of an organization (Weber, 1947). It is a rationalized form of power accomplished and enforced through procedural requirements seemingly impervious to the particularity of unique or individual desires. Thus, a bureaucratic structure is one that governs itself and others by making use of established protocols and procedures – these are usually put into text as rules and regulations implemented by an office in a supposedly predictable fashion. These rule-guided procedures, which aim to regularize the management of all members of an organization, can be understood as definitive of bureaucracy's capacity to wrest power from the control of individual interests and influence. Paradoxically, it is this depersonalized character of bureaucratic management that can be understood as its key valued feature as well as its most intractable problem.

The paradox of bureaucracy, conceived of as protection against personal arbitrariness while also inhibiting an organization's capacity to be responsive to the essentially irregular character that is human life, points to the necessity of developing a critical approach. Given its paradoxical character, improving bureaucracy does not necessarily undo the fact that its desired outcome is simultaneously its barrier-riddled limit. Improved bureaucratic order can end up enhancing the paradox all the more.

The paradox of bureaucracy is not only a confounding quandary that courses through modernity. It is also a prevalent productive force constituting conceptions of regular procedures, normal participants, and typical processes as these are formed over and against the abnormal, the troublesome, or the exceptional. Bureaucratic processes define how regular participation and activities will be accomplished, and they also define the normal, routine order of its accomplishment. This means that the paradox of bureaucracy is one that produces forms of subjectivity, such as the good worker, student, or recipient of services, or the citizen and the immigrant. Bureaucracy constitutes forms of belonging as well as the parameters of normal participation. What does not fit is encapsulated as an exception to the rule (Agamben, 2005; Michalko, 2002; Overboe, 1999). Sherene Razack's (2010) work on matters of race, for example, demonstrates that the state of exception courses through all bureaucratic space. Disability is defined by (and for) bureaucracy as an inability to perform in a way that is considered normal for a human due to a limitation in function or structure, and it is thus already conceived of as such an exception (WHO, 1980).

How, then, to develop an inquiry that can grapple with the social implications of bureaucracy's paradoxical character as it frames questions of the relations between bodies and social space? The work of social and political theorists, inclusive of anti-racist studies, leads the way towards the necessity of grappling with power as it operates through bureaucratic processes. Bureaucracy is a key form of modern governance insofar as it has enabled, enhanced, and even enforced the workings of capitalism, neo-liberal ideology, settler mentalities, and colonialist enterprises. Bureaucracy, understood as dominating the management of bodies and social space, is thus an important arena for research for disability studies. While revealing disability's tie to bureaucratic management, we can also address bureaucratic management's paradoxical power to make disability an unmanageable state of exception in the university environment.

Disability Studies

Treating both demands for and denials of access as an occasion to wonder about the current set-up of daily life involves a kind of transformation of consciousness regarding access and disabled people. But it is not, for example, the absence of accessibility features in my workplace that has made access a growing concern; those absences have been prevalent for a very long time not only in my workplace but also in most workplaces and indeed in most environments. What is bringing the relations between bodies and social space to consciousness in new ways is, in part, the emerging field of *disability studies.*

Disability studies is an academic, activist, and artistic endeavour that aims to make us attend to, and even rethink, the way we imagine, perceive, and treat disability and disabled people (Titchkosky and Michalko, 2009). During the past few years, I have developed and taught disability studies courses, conducted disability studies research, consulted with and supervised graduate students' work in disability studies, and have all the while engaged with access issues. In the midst of these various experiences, I have come to realize that little is straightforward in the quest for access, and even less is certain in the meaning of the relation between embodiment and social space. People are starting to wonder about access; how it is rejected; how it is blocked; and how it is represented, as well as by whom. This wondering is making a difference to how the idea of access is accessed. In the midst of all sorts of inaccessible features of university life, disability studies is also becoming part of various academic environments, including at the university where I work. On the cusp of a perceptual transformation, access as a social issue and disability as a non-individualized matter are gaining some prevalence and legitimacy in my workplace. Access is becoming something to think about.

Access is, of course, both a very new and a very old concern. From a disability studies perspective, what access actually means – its social significance – is a captivating endeavour. The study of this meaning can change how we do things, since it requires reflection on what is being made of disability, bodies, and social space. After all, how people actually attend to, and orient to, access influences not only the relations among people but also the basic meaning of people. Disability studies is a new form of perception, both because of its tie to activist pursuits and because the theoretical work that arises from it offers yet another relation between bodies and social space – namely, a self-reflective one. This, too, is part of, and acts on, the social environment.

I treat my experience in the university environment as an opportunity to access 'access' as a form of oriented social action; it is a form of consciousness which is providing for the possibility of engaging access as a meaningful space within which to question the organization of social life, especially in its bureaucratic configurations. Disability studies attends to the appearance of disability and non-disability as social and political expressions. Access procedures, policy development, discussions, and arguments in the round of university life are some of the ways disability and non-disability come to make an appearance. Still, this appearance is complicated. Consider, for example, how ordinary introductory web material regarding student accommodation at the University of Toronto makes access a scene that produces the meaning of people and places.

Accessibility Services, St George Campus

What We Do

The role of Accessibility Services is to facilitate the inclusion of students with disabilities into all aspects of university life. Our focus is on skills development, especially in the areas of self-advocacy and academic skills.

Services are provided to students with a documented disability. It can be physical, sensory, a learning disability, or a mental health disorder. Students with temporary disabilities (e.g. broken arm) are also eligible for the service. (http://www.accessibility.utoronto.ca/about.htm, accessed April 13, 2010)

There is nothing extraordinary about this statement and ones like it can be found in centres and offices that provide services for 'students with disabilities' in many universities. For example, on the Disability Resource Centre website at the University of Calgary, we read:

The Disability Resource Centre (DRC) works with students, faculty and staff to facilitate an accessible learning environment for students with disabilities. We work with students who have permanent disabilities

(i.e., life-long or chronic) and those with temporary impairments
(i.e., medical conditions) to identify reasonable academic accommodations that will support them in achieving their academic goals . . . From the
time they enter the University of Calgary, students with documented disabilities can benefit from our services. Every student registered with the
Disability Resource Centre meets with an advisor to review their individual learning needs and how their disability impacts the learning process.
(http://www.ucalgary.ca/ses/services/drc/, accessed April 10, 2010)

Similar in tone and content, here is another 'welcome and mission'
statement that addresses disability and access issues. This statement
comes from a small, primarily undergraduate university:

Welcome to the website for the Program for Students with Disabilities.
The main goals of our program are to assist students in transferring effec-
tive learning strategies to the university environment and to develop the
working partnerships they need to be successful. The fundamental approach of St. Francis Xavier University stresses the development of self-
advocacy and independence for students with disabilities. The University
promotes awareness, advocacy and learning partnerships among students
with disabilities and the whole university community . . . (http://www.
stfx.ca/campus/stu-serv/disabled-students/, accessed April 10, 2009)

The very ordinariness and unified consistency of these expressions of
access issues and accommodation procedures across a nation should
give us a reason to reflect. Welcoming students is accomplished by inviting them to share in the understanding that inclusion is a mission
achieved through the enhancement of individual skills. Self-advocacy
and academic skill enhancement are services provided to those with
a documented disability and such services are to be understood as a
legitimate, even invitational, way to be oriented to the mission of inclusion. Understanding disability as a personal need which requires
evaluation, services, or counseling, rather than collective action or exploration, requires us to engage disability in individualized terms.

What has this 'ordinary access' talk and conduct given us access
to? It tells us, for the purposes of accommodation services, *who* disabled students are: they are people in need of enhancement due to a
documented disability which is impairing their full inclusion. *What* the
problem is, then, is disability as an individual matter. Disability is the
location of trouble since it results in the difficulty of having one's needs

met, as well as potentially causing academic problems and barriers to learning. *Where* this mission is brought to fruition is in the individual life of the student seeking accessibility services. Skill acquisition, be it academic or advocacy oriented, is the manifestation of the accessibility services mission. *When* the student's disability is documented (certified by a medical practitioner) and the student registers with accessibility services, they become part of the history of the mission of inclusion configured not so much as a right or a collective desire, but as a project yet to be completed. Thus, we have been given an understanding of disability access issues as a thoroughly individualized matter. Disability accommodation services begin with the mission of converting people with a documented disability into people who understand that seeking skill enhancement through the correct office, and in respect to the appropriate rules, is the way to potentially secure their inclusion in education and perhaps the wider society. Nonetheless, disability is ensconced as an individual trouble that makes a person not fully at one with the workings of university life. Ironically, these access mission statements individualize disability and yet they themselves are far from individual missions.

Access is not just a word that indicates a lack of inclusion; it is also a way of perceiving, talking, and acting. 'I need access.' 'I don't have access!' 'I am not what they say I am, but I got access to what I need from them.' 'Now, now I've got it, I'm in.' Such phrases can trick us into thinking that access is the substance, the end point, the object of concern. But access is not really a substance and it is more than a process. As perception, as talk and conduct, as a form of consciousness, access leads us to ask how access can be an interpretive move that puts people into different kinds of relations with their surroundings. Anything said about access can be read for how it reflects a host of questions: Who has access? Access to where? Access to what? When? Every single instance of life can be regarded as tied to access – that is, to do anything is to have some form of access. This is an important issue to address in relation to those who are expected and enabled by the social environment, and thus appear as non-disabled and as though they are unconnected to access concerns. The question now becomes: How is it that we regard some aspects of everyday life as an access concern and others as not? If we engage access and disability issues by raising such questions, we gain the possibility of learning something new about the culture from which these issues spring and to which these issues return for rejoinder.

The Five W's

The chapters in this book consist of explorations into the interpretive scenes that make up questions of access and, thus, the meaning of disability. Each chapter, or scene, is also a way to focus on and pursue one of the 'W5' questions: who, what, where, when, and why?

Chapter 2 addresses how access as an interpretive activity gives rise to questions regarding *who* belongs and, in belonging, how legitimate identities are forged. Questions regarding *what* is being communicated by common symbolic representations of access, such as the white wheelchair icon on blue background, is the scene explored in chapter 3. That chapter includes an examination of what we are doing and what we are making of disability when we represent it through icons of access, through person-first language, and through other narratives.

The scene of the question 'where?' is taken up in chapter 4. It addresses the seemingly bizarre 'inclusion of disability as an excludable type' (Titchkosky, 2007a) by analysing the mundane, everyday ways in which this process of in/exclusion is made to seem normal and ordinary. Workplace narratives that aim to justify a lack of access, and how this gives rise to questions of *where* we find ourselves in an imagined experience of our bodies, is the scene explored in chapter 4.

In chapter 5, I examine some of the historical consequences of configuring disability as an excludable type. In addressing the question of 'when?' this chapter represents what Elizabeth Grosz (2003: 13) calls 'a history of the present' by exploring access issues as they appear in current university policy and in more activist scenes of interaction. The issue of when access becomes a question – and when it does not – is interrogated for grounding conceptions of disability that govern ideas of participation and images of belonging. I am particularly interested in how disability is socially produced as something that is not yet considered an essential participant in social life. Still, including disability as excludable is a scene where the meaning of the concept of 'all people' is forged.

The final chapter addresses the fifth W, the question of 'why?' but, hopefully, in an unexpected manner. Even though I ask 'why?' I do not do so as an attempt to explain disability's non-participation. Explaining non-participation requires us to confirm a conception of disability that allows for non-participation in the first place. So, instead, I *question the question* of 'why?' and this leads to a reflection on the desire to ask the question, to attempt to explain non-participation, in the first place. Such a reflection points us towards the possibility of a different question – the question of *how* we come to perceive the legitimacy of exclusion and inclusion. Turning to the question of how – how we do what we do, how we include and exclude – changes the task of inquiry from one which tries to explain, and thus control, what can be known, to one whose task it is to understand what appears and, in this understanding, orient to new possible scenes of questions.

Following Henri-Jacques Stiker's (1999: 18) methodological imperative to '. . . enlarge the understanding that we already have,' this book aims to understand how disability and access make an appearance in university life. I do not investigate disability access issues *with* the W5 questions; instead, I regard the issue of access as representative *of* such questions, and try to enlarge our present understanding of these questions with hopes of being moved to the point of wonder. Such wondering marks the occasion to question conceptions of who belongs and how, as well as what appearing and belonging to the category of disability represents. Further, we ask ourselves: Where in the built environment do questions arise regarding participation, and how do these questions arise?

Politics of Wonder

The socially accomplished meaning of disability and access is not best addressed by a cause/effect empirical rationality. Coming face-to-face with questions of meaning requires not explanation, but rather explorations of that which grounds what is already said and already done. Resisting the dominant 'why?' question is done in support of my goal to come to a more explicit development of a *politics of wonder*. Moving from 'why?' to 'how?' invites a politics open to wonder – a wondering about that which organizes bodies and social spaces and their worlds of meaning. I make use of what I call a restless reflexive return to what has come before. This requires us to be restless with the concept of certainty by returning to its production and not permitting it to remain unquestionably certain. That is, the certainty of knowledge regarding disability and access must be examined as a way to uncover how this certainty is produced and sustained. Such questioning culminates in a 'politics of wonder' – a wondering oriented to exploring the possibility of disability and disability studies.

Scenes of access are opportunities to address questions such as *who* belongs and how; *what* do representations of disability mean; *when* does an interest in disability become elided so as to not yet figure as a necessary participant; and *where* does all this happen? These questions, of course, are asked in the spaces of everyday life which are organized by taken-for-granted relations to who and what belongs, for whom and when. This leads us to ask if we might come to know disability differently by wondering about how people have already come to know disability with certainty. In contemporary Western workplace environments, for example, people recognize and know disability with certainty; such workplaces are therefore spaces where, through a politics of wonder, we might gain access to knowing disability differently.

Any time access is spoken about or acted upon is an opportunity to reveal how access is a form of perception and thus a space of questions. For example, a common expression that arises as people struggle to secure physical access is, 'Look, disability just wasn't a concern when this building was built.' 'Look' is a recent expression which does the interactional work of pointing out what should be obvious and beyond question. Still, this declaration of certainty hosts many questions. Who are 'we' such that disabled people are excluded? Who are disabled people such that 'they' can be overlooked in the past? Who do we become when such a past is used as a justification for the present state of affairs? How might the space we find in our workplace socially organize what is thinkable and doable there? How is it that what access means for you and what it means for me are different, and what might these different interpretations do for inclusion, for exclusion, and the intermingling of the two? Finally, that we are asked – told, actually – to 'look' at the issue one way implies it could be understood in other ways. If the ordinary sentiment that 'disability just wasn't a concern when this building was built' contains so much to think about, then it is no wonder that we need now to wonder about access as it makes an appearance in university life. Instead of developing explanations, plans, or rationalizations, a politics of wonder returns to what is already demanded, ensconced, or explained, since what has been done contains what people already mean to and for each other.

Reflecting on, and thus re-engaging, the place of existing meanings makes possible something other than the repetition of more of the same. A restless return permits us to wonder about what is already said and done – and it is political to the extent that it can forge new imaginative relations to what is already well-established, powerful, and serving as the taken-for-granted constitutive grounds of future action, thought, movement, and feeling. A politics of wonder allows us to remake our lives together by wondering about the shape they hold and the meaning already ascribed to them. A more traditional social science procedure would require the identification of problems, the development of an explanatory theory as to the problems' causes, and the development of solutions. In contrast, the approach here puts the identification of problems, the explanation of said problems, and the development of solutions all on the same level. All these activities are the stuff of social life in regard to which the theoretic imagination needs to return and to wonder, 'How *is* "what is" accomplished and what does it mean?'[3]

But disability seems to be a fact of life in regard to which very little room is granted for wondering and theorizing, and doing so may even seem inappropriate. One of the most common approaches to disability is to conceive of it as biologically grounded and explainable as such, and to seek solutions in order to cure, care for, or contain disability. Since the time that 'the disabled' were first constituted as the 'deserving poor' during the Enlightenment's biomedical management of growing urban populations (Davis, 1995; Foucault, 1978; Zola, 1977), disability has been mercilessly subjected to the 'why?' question and has thus become, to put it bluntly, too well known. Today, disability is very well known as something gone wrong and is often represented as embodied wrongness. In fact, disability today is so singularly well known as the space of unwanted calamity in need of cure, care, or containment that it has become the space *par excellence* for the ongoing workings of colonialism, state management, and the governing of modern versions of selfhood (Finkelstein, 1998; Titchkosky and Aubrecht, 2009). Disability is so taken-for-granted as unwanted, an unnecessary problem – and, as Rod Michalko (2002) has shown, constituted as a 'useless difference' – that disability is today the space where there seems to be almost unlimited permission for the powers that be to go in and deal with 'the disabled.' This unlimited permission to deal with disability seems especially true in regard to anything understood as a mental, intellectual, or developmental impairment. We can also come to programmatic relations with access too quickly, where we simply know too much, and this occurs in activist as well as in academic realms. When it seems to us that the only thing that matters is the fight for access as *though* this fight is not also constitutive of the meaning of people and places, we risk participating in the current regimes which know disability too well. To know disability without needing to wonder about this knowledge is to risk re-achieving the containment of bodies in social spaces, thus disallowing a growing and creative sense of alternative embodiments. Doing right or achieving rights without a politics of wonder are not risks that we should be willing to take. Under modern conditions of global capitalism, where disability is consistently regarded as a problem, a politics of wonder can help dissuade us from a tyranny of containment that is achieved by current dominant knowledge regimes and through which devastating control is held.

We need a politics of wonder that allows us to reflect on the sort of problem we already understand disability to be. What we do to disability includes a forced management of people, communities, and entire countries – for example, enforced drugging of individuals through community treatment orders; the United Nations' demand for countries to spend more on Western mental health and illness medication; environmental emergency preparedness protocols that include making some bodies less worthy of saving than others; rehabilitation and health programs that regard disability as only a personal problem unrelated to discriminatory social structures and interpretations; genomic, health, and fitness regimes that normalize the *pursuit* of the normal body; the over-representation of racialized, First Nation or Roma children in categories of learning disabilities; or the plethora of discourses that regard disability as a living death, void of creative potential. Since the advent of totalitarianism (Arendt, 1973; Bauman, 2000, 2004), anything that seems so 'totally knowable,' and so clearly in need of banal bureaucratic management justified as medically necessary, should give us pause to wonder. In order to conceive of disability differently (Michalko, 1998, 2002; Titchkosky, 2007b), it is necessary to ask what we are doing when we 'do things' to disability and to disabled people. A politics of wonder has the potential to make us regard embodied interpretive relations as a place where people develop the capacity to question by revealing the questions that are already there.

I turn now to a narrative that illustrates how I will proceed in developing a politics of wonder while also serving to narrate my own position in relation to questions of access and disability. In the following I consider my experiences with access in order to wonder about what is at stake when access comes up as a question in university life.

Half and Half[4]

I invite you to begin where I do; as I write this, I am situated in the midst of a variety of half-and-half experiences. I have spent half of my time in university as a student and the other half as a professor. Being 'middle-aged' marks, at least in my imagination, a halfway point in my life; and, part-way through my career after nearly a decade of teaching at one university, I am starting over at a new university; so, I am half established and half new. As a disability studies scholar, I am a welcomed member of my new university but I am also within an environment which has few ways to imagine disabled participants; I am doing, representing, and arguing for the inclusion of disability as it appears both half in and half out; half marginal and now also a part of the mainstream.

In the midst of all these halfway marks, I have now also spent half of my life as a dyslexic, and the other half as . . . well, as something else. My being something else, my other half of life, has been variously characterized as lazy, inattentive, as not applying myself, not smart, as not caring, not right, a little messed up, mixed up, too slow and too quick, as basically having literacy problems that, often, make me a problem.[5] So, my time as dyslexic marks a halfway point in my life, too; half in and half out; half marginal and half mainstream.

But what is not half-and-half is my need to take a little more time to do things such as follow instructions, remember, learn dates, names, places; a little more time to tell the time; a little more time to grade, to write, to read and practice reading. I need a little more time to figure things out, to wonder about how normal things are done in normal ways. Half of the time I spend working with, and the other half coping with, being dyslexic, and this dyslexia has marked me as having a rather intimate relation to print culture. My relation to print culture also comes in the shape of a half-and-half, since I either have difficulties when I take print culture for granted or I find it difficult to do so. To be of this culture, I also need to study it and, in this way, dyslexia denaturalizes the social life of literacy (Titchkosky, 2005, 2008b). Yet, another half-and-half resides here; my literacy competency, like most competencies, is tied to acting as if the social life of literacy is natural, as if I am not half and half but, instead, fully at one with it (Ferri and Connor, 2006; Jenkins, 1998). My dyslexia puts me in a half-and-half relation even in the face of a desire to be at one with print culture (Heap, 1991; Meek, 1992).

Interestingly enough, noticing that one is positioned as half-and-half provides different kinds of access to everyday life. For example, in my half-and-half account, we now have access to at least three relations to time: time is a starting point – 'At the point of writing this book'; time is a narrative measure – 'my time as half-and-half . . .'; and time is a substance used to do things like start on projects and forge histories of ourselves – or to tell you a story about dyslexia as it appears over time. Bureaucratic institutions sometimes like to believe that they follow but one sense of time – objective, linear, ordinary time – and when accommodations are sought in the university it is this sort of time that students may receive. For example, 'I get time-and-a-half to write this exam.' Some institutions and some of their members even pretend that this version of time, like literacy, is not political but is instead 'natural.' The naturalization of the stuff of culture can make it appear that receiving 'time-and-a-half to write an exam' is an unfair personal advantage. Conceiving of time as if given by nature may serve to disallow people from perceiving how academic accommodations are an institutional attempt to be responsive to human diversity and difference. This is necessitated by a very exclusive version of time that moves in only one direction and in only one way for people at all times. But this is also a myth of our times.

There are many senses of time, there are many ways we refer to time, and there are many different ways to 'do' time. Through these three relations to time (as starting point, as measure, as narrative substance), my story is made to make sense. It is that there are at least three sorts of time that allows me to say the following, 'At this *time*, let me *take a minute* to tell you what happened when I could not *tell the time* and the class went *overtime* and I made all of us *late.* ' So positioned in time, in our lives as half-and-half, we can invite thinking about our always partially positioned relations to the seemingly certain nature of social life, including the movements of time.

Recognizing this half-and-half position marks a return to the sort of time that seems to be more full but more restless. This is the sort of time that is less like a linear march forward and more reflective of the stuff of life. I am referring to the sort of time which includes a sense of relations with friends and families; with health issues, disability, poverty, nation; a reflexive sense of the processes of racializing, gendering, and sexualizing of people; time structured by the power relations of the bureaucratic moves of late capitalism – all of which, together and in conflict, make up the complex time/space nexus of daily life. This return to the time of the social organization of everyday life, a return to what people have already said and done, is an invitation to parcel some time together into an experience of being half and half.

Proceeding through a half-and-half relation to self and to others, I do not mean beginning as a bunch of happy dyslexics who now know what skills we need to learn in order to get done what we wish. This is not just about understanding our personal learning needs and confidently wielding self-advocacy skills. By half and half, I don't mean accepting the things that limit us – such as not driving, not spelling well, not knowing left from right, not getting rules, directions, or instructions straight; needing a little more of that bureaucratic linear time that can feel so much like 'doing' time; and, in all these potential differences, risk not appearing competent. Nor do I mean the half-measures and half-attempts that collectives develop in order to deal with bodies, minds, senses, and emotions understood as different. I don't mean the half-attempts to address the different life histories that run up against discord in the meaningful places of everyday life, such as universities and their requirements and reward structures that are based on unquestioned 'skill' sets. All of us do have particular differences which we are learning to, or struggling to, live with . . . but this is not what I mean when I say let us begin as half and half.

Beginning from a lesson generated from the experience of disability is to begin knowing that we are a part of and apart from – that we are made by and we make – the space where we find ourselves. Half and half is a metaphoric way to refer to being guided by the understanding that we are both apart from and a part of that which makes us: culture. 'Culture' is a term that reminds us that we live in, through, and with others and their interpretive material realities. Recognizing that it is possible to conceive of 'positionality' as a half and half is also the grounds on which we find ourselves. Made by culture, we have good reason to return to the spaces of that making; the possibility of this return lies in the fact that we are not at 'one' with culture, since we do not simply mirror that which we are both a part of and apart from. Being not one, but half and half, sustains what I earlier called a restless reflexive return. This return makes it more difficult to pretend that the appearance of dyslexia, or of any other disability, happens outside of socially structured exclusions that are bureaucratically ordered by the hyper-literacy requirements of modern Westernized worlds. Without mass literacy demands, there is no dyslexia; with dyslexia, there arises something other than a person fully at one with literate culture. We are both subjects of culture and those who can forge new relations to it.

We are all, in some sense, half and half – a part of and apart from where we find ourselves. This always has something to say about the meaning of persons, both collectively and individually. Even when the people who we may assume ourselves to be are quite opposite to what others assume us to be, this still means that part of who we are is tied to knowing something about what or who *we are not*. In the global disability rights movement, it is commonly said that 'We are people!' or 'I am a person first!' Half of what such sayings are doing is asserting the neo-liberal status of modern conceptions of the human. The other half of what people-first language does is reflect the taken-for-granted assumption that disability lacks legitimacy as a way of being human. In insisting that 'I am a person first,' disability is once again formed as a condition attached to persons. Disability is stigmatized and assumed to be not quite human, not quite at one with how contemporary life has imagined the so-called human (Goffman, 1963: 5; Garland-Thomson, 1997; Titchkosky, 2000). Not all people, after all, need to assert their status as human.[6]

Let us also consider some other highly structured identity categories of university life: 'student,' 'staff,' and 'faculty.' These are the three general categories of persons who, like the category 'person with a disability,' are structured by being part of and apart from the university; that which makes them what they are and makes the space in which they find themselves. Being a student, for example, is being a part of an organized educational system *but* it also means being a part of something else. It is to be partly something other than what is expected by its 'ready-made' social location (Taylor, 1989; Michalko, 2002). Being a student and participating in student life are part of each other but not at one with each other. Every identity category carries some constitutive relation to what it is not (Graham and Slee, 2008). Half of what I am writing here is simply a return to what everybody already knows, namely, that they *are* 'not that.' The other half involves thinking and theorizing about how we might live with what we already know. The question of how to live with the understanding that people are positioned in a half-and-half relation to culture *is* an orientation to being half and half.

Orienting to Half and Half

The question, now, is how to live with being half and half. Social theorist Zygmunt Bauman (2004: 20) can be read to put the matter of living as half and half this way:

> The idea of identity was born out of the crisis of belonging and out of the effort it triggered to bridge the gap between the 'ought' and the 'is' – to remake the reality in the likeness of the idea.

Bauman is suggesting that we belong half to conceptions of what we ought to be and half to conceptions of what we already are. But he also says that '[t]he idea of identity was born out of a crisis of belonging . . .' My crisis of belonging can happen when I stop fully identifying as inattentive, lazy, uncaring, or as one who has a problem and thus is a problem. What 'is' is that I have been regarded as being a problem by others and by myself; what 'ought to be' is that it ought to be otherwise. Between this *is* and this *ought,* a crisis of belonging arises. In general, disability or any embodied difference 'is' identified negatively. As disability studies scholar Paul Abberley (1998: 93) tells us, disabled people are often only 'relevant' or interesting as problems. Yet a crisis of identity arises when we begin to believe that what *is* 'ought' to be otherwise. People cannot question identity, or make identity, unless there is a crisis of belonging, of being in and out, that goes on to trigger a crisis of consciousness wherein we know we are positioned between what ought to be and what is. We are not a singular, unified self at one with where we find ourselves. In this recognition of an essential split or rupture in being lie both conflict and the potential for building something new.

Reflecting on our actual existence as half and half, neither fully determined nor undetermined by culture, is the foundation for the movement of critical thought on what has already been produced as meaningful relations between bodies and spaces. For example, as dyslexic, I need more time to accomplish the activities of daily literacy. This experience gives me access to different relations with time – and even if I have, in the end, less time, I also have a more nuanced relation to the fullness of time as I reflect on the crisis between how time is and how it ought to be. Time is more and other than how it conventionally appears. While my time as dyslexic is sometimes less than pleasant, especially when linear time appears as a demanding convention which I have failed to grasp – let alone follow – it is also wondrously interesting when time is denaturalized and reveals something of its everyday uses and order. Moreover, that my need for time marks me as a person in need, or even as one who fails to appear in the cloak of normalcy, gives us access to time as a space where we can question what we mean to each other.

This lesson of needing to think from the position of half and half is a lesson from a discipline that I have had much difficulty with – namely, mathematics. From my position of easily mixing up numbers, I have also learned just how important numerical order is. Here, too, we can receive the sense that even the discipline of mathematics might know something of the subjective experience of being half and half. Why do you want to know the number, the angle, the measurement of something, unless you know it could be otherwise? And, in this vein, why might you want to know the angle of the door in relation to the sink and grab bar, unless you have already begun to imagine other possible angles to identify in the environment? A different sort of identity issue lies here which, nonetheless, arises from the act of noticing that there is a difference between what is and what ought to be. To make use of Bauman again, the likeness of the idea of an accessible washroom becomes recognizable through the process of measurement, especially when we attend to the crisis between what is and what ought to be. This example demonstrates that any conception of faculty, student, or staff, or any university discipline or event, can open us to the possibility that things could be otherwise. Yet every aspect of university work and life can also close us from this lesson. Half and half is a metaphor to express that people are not the same as that which grounds their possibility and that the goings-on of everyday life are other than how they first appear.

Half In and Half Out

I will now turn more directly to the example of disability and questions of access in order to explore what we might learn from the social fact that it is possible to claim – even embrace – a half-and-half position in university life. Access, addressed as the gap between what is and what ought to be, can lead to questions that arise in the gap between the experience of learning, physical, psychic, or sensory disabilities, and the particular environment where this learning occurs.

To identify as a disabled student, staff, or faculty member in most universities today is to be confronted with questions of access. The intellectual, physical, electronic, and all other aspects of the university environment make participation by disabled people questionable. The identity of disabled people on campuses is inscribed at every turn with a big question mark. At every set of stairs, at every location without an elevator or accessible washroom or with an obstacle-strewn ramp, at every 'teaching moment' that enforces only one singular way of learning, educational environments inscribe our bodies and our lives into the shape of a question. What does this mean?

Who are you? We weren't expecting you! I mean, I know you said you were coming, but still I didn't think you would actually show up. You know, you are disabled, after all?!

And there are more questions that the presence of disability has been made to represent –

> Who are you? We weren't expecting you! You know, don't you, this place is not set up for you? It is not as if the structures and intentions of the university environment are about to change for the sake of a few students and their so-called differences . . . Change takes time and it, I mean you, I mean it, simply costs too much. You must realize how much it would cost to include disability? But maybe, maybe, we could change you. A little technology, or perhaps a bursary? Time-and-a-half? Or maybe you should consider going part-time. And if that doesn't make you just the same as everybody else . . . Could you go ahead and do the full-time job of being a disabled member in this environment on your own time? Surely you understand that you are not in synch with this. No harm meant, it is just that this building, this program, was not designed with you in mind.

Being half and half, our embodied differences function also as a question to those who question disability's presence. The presence of disability, like disability studies, gives rise to a question, which was articulated by Irving Zola many years ago when disability studies was just starting to emerge on the North American university scene. Zola (1982: 244) asked, 'How has a society been created and perpetuated which has excluded so many of its members?'

That being disabled means facing questions of access is not something new; it is a lesson that the Union Against the Segregation of the Physically Impaired (UPIAS), in the UK, has been teaching for more than thirty years. Since 1975, the Social Model of Disability flowing from UPIAS's work (1976: 4) has been reminding us as follows:

> Our own position on disability is quite clear . . . it is society which disables physically impaired people. Disability is something imposed on top of our impairments, by the way we are unnecessarily isolated and excluded from full participation in society. Disabled people are therefore an oppressed group in society.

We ought to know this, and whoever does not know this may have a difficult time learning it now. We know there are buildings traversed by thousands of people every day that are void of ramps, void of a single accessible washroom, void of any imagination regarding who belongs. We know, too, that there are the blue and white wheelchair access signs posted on all sorts of inaccessible, quasi- or partially-accessible features within the North American university environment. We know there are rules, regulations, and structures of education that bar access to anything, except for the most ordinary of participants shadowing the ghosts and illusions of normalcy. University buildings are also filled to capacity with unnecessary acts of exclusion. Against the illusion of one way of learning, of one education, of one type of student, and of one type of teacher all under one set of administrative rules, let us return to the ambiguity of being half and half.

Many physical and social environments are set up as if they never imagined the incredible variety of bodies, minds, senses, emotions, and lives that are 'us.' Daily life seems instead to function with a mythical, singular conception of the typical human, or what feminist disability studies scholar Rosemarie Garland-Thomson (1997: 7) refers to as 'normate man.' Normate is a way to describe the typically unmarked category of persons that are culturally positioned as expected, and are thus taken as definitive human beings. A belief in normate man and normate culture helps to make the marginalization, or even exclusion, of some people seem natural. This process is perpetuated by the removal of definitional power from those understood as disabled. Daily life confronts many people as an obstacle to participation since it is set up in support of this mythical normate man.

University life makes many of its members, or potential members, into a presence that is not imagined, not welcomed, and yet . . . we are here. Or, here we are, the unimagined in flesh and blood. There is a strange, inverted proportionality in this ambiguously related half and half: inasmuch as society fails to respond to impairments and other social differences, such as race, ethnicity, sexuality, and gender – and inasmuch as embodiment is organized by social life – we are also part of this life. Being positioned as 'out' has something to do with the social organization of embodiment that is 'in.'

UPIAS's reference to the process of disablement, whereby the 'unnecessarily isolated and excluded' are constructed, is generated from a complex web of social activity that entails the production of something more than isolation and exclusion. People are positioned differently in relation to the social production of marginality. Some people are positioned as isolated and needing to respond collectively to isolation; others are positioned as excluded and needing to include this sense of exclusion into the workings of everyday life. This is an irony that comes to the fore when we attend to a half-and-half positionality. It is the irony of the structures of an in/out dichotomy; the construction of who is out is intimately tied to who is in, and as we work at getting in, the production of who and what is out continues (Bauman, 1990; Berger, 1963; Butler, 2009; Corker, 2001). We are a part of university life in a strange, inverted way, since we are questioning the norms of access that have made participation questionable. Examining being left out is also a way of getting in – and strangely enough, this examination shows that, unlike us, 'normate man' never shows up in the flesh. As disability historian Henri-Jacques Stiker (1999: 51) says, 'We are always other than what society made us and believes us to be.' People are made by that which excludes and are more than that. This is what the metaphor of being half and half represents.

Through the image of a wheelchair user being confronted by a flight of stairs, or an inaccessible washroom, or a walkway with no curb cut, we come face-to-face with exclusion. This is certainly a failure of access. But from the position of half and half, the confrontation between people and their exclusions also includes a living reproach, a living critique, of environmental limits. It is, however, not easy to face the crisis of identity at the base of those stairs, or outside the washroom, where we are positioned between what is (exclusion) and what ought to be (inclusion and more). Between the 'ought' and the 'is' is a person living with the likeness of the idea of belonging (Michalko, 2002: 167). At the base of those stairs or in the washroom with no grab bar, all people are positioned half as those who perpetuate exclusion (what is) and half as those who might notice exclusion (what ought to be). How, then, does a community develop a relation to a cultural demand that situates disability – and all sorts of other social differences now being managed under disability designations – as partial participants who are individually expected to work towards gaining human status in a human-made world? How does a community develop the need to reflectively remake what has been passing as human in the first place, and thus do something other than shore up the boundaries around a limited version of personhood?

We (disabled people) are excluded, even unimagined, and we know that getting in is tied to the production of who and what is out. But how do we live in the midst of these tensions? Half of the battle is the fight for access; the other half is the need to think about or question what we have indeed been given access to. *If we are half out we are also half in and if we are half in we need to ask what we are 'in for.'* Thus, the development of dynamic learning communities needs a half-and-half relation to itself – that is, to the questions of access – if it is to renew itself, or do something other than reproduce more of the same. It must recognize that the need for a half-and-half relation to where people find themselves is different from the need to make plans for future change. It is the need to return to what people and places already do and say as a way to generate a crisis of identity so that it is not as easy to imagine some people as unintended participants. Talk and action regarding access can be regarded as the place for a critical pursuit of what access is already giving us access to, a place where the ready-made dichotomies of in/out, self/other, and so on, can be addressed. Living in the midst of the tension of a half-and-half position provides for the possibility of not only recognizing exclusion and demanding inclusion, but also uncovering and understanding how the exclusion that is identified can be included into a yet-to-be-imagined world that promises something other than the same.

Disability studies poet and activist Eli Clare says,

> I want us to cruise justice, flirt with it, take it home with us, nurture and feed it, even though sometimes it will be demanding and uncomfortable and ask us to change. Clearly I'm not talking about a simple one night stand but a commitment for the long haul. (Clare, 2002: n.p.)

Clare suggests that justice is not something that we are or something that we have; it is instead a relation. We can cruise, flirt, and try to live with justice because we are not at one with it. Justice, then, is not a synonym for access. Or, access can, at most, be only part of what justice means. The fight for access is the beginning of living more intimately with the interpretive material reality which has perpetuated so much exclusion; therefore, access initiatives come with the uncomfortable task of needing to ask, 'What does inclusion mean?' Treating access as an end point does not demonstrate the 'long haul' commitment of which Clare speaks. Fights for access necessarily invite us to get more intimate with mainstream existence, and thus more intimate with the exclusionary prowess that makes the struggle necessary in the first place. To get any more intimate with in/exclusion, we need to nurture our need for justice by not being at one with the answers that become secure along the way.

The fight for the rights to access may get people in – but that is only half the issue. Developing critical relations to access that are committed to recognizing how it already interprets embodied difference is the other half. With the growing realization that the physical and social environment has everything to do with how we can and cannot live, in our particular ways, as embodied beings, this book recommends continued questioning as a necessary political response and responsibility. It is this questioning that *is* the community we are now developing. Still, how to become such questioners?

In order to question the status, orders, and organizations of university life, I turn now to a consideration of how people are given access to very ordinary and exclusionary conceptions of disability in the time and place of the university. Orienting to such a question has much to do with 'who' we are.

2 'Who?': Disability Identity and the Question of Belonging

Questions such as Who are you? Who are you to me? Who am I to you? arise in talk and conduct surrounding access in universities today. My interest in this chapter is about access as a question of *who belongs*. Through an analysis of ordinary access talk occurring in my place of work at the University of Toronto, this chapter explores how lines are drawn around belongingness, especially as this relates to access and participation in university life.

I begin by reflecting on a particular interaction where the question of who belongs was raised in such a way as to actually dismiss the possibility that disabled people belong. This interaction was explicitly discriminatory, but the question of 'who belongs?' also arises in more subtle, everyday ways. Questions regarding who belongs arise for multiple reasons, even seemingly progressive ones such as identity politics or as a way to achieve polite recognition. In order to theorize the constitution of legitimate participants, I consider 'who?' questions that arise within bureaucratically managed educational life under late capitalism. How the 'who?' question arises in the face of the identification of disability is regarded here as an interactional scene, critical for rethinking who we are to and for one another.

Exploring some of the ways of depicting who disabled people are supposed to be will provide access to the social practice of drawing boundaries around forms of participation. 'Who?' serves as a space of questions that draws boundaries around who is in and who is out; this is not only demonstrated here but also theorized so that we can wonder about what it means to transform the question of 'who are you?' into the question 'who belongs?' as this reflects the interests of organizations and communities. Thus, I show that disability is a space where it is possible to gain access to the social meaning of being human and, perhaps, begin to make this version of human otherwise than ordinary.

Living the Question of 'Who?'

'Who?' she said.

Yes, the university person responsible for space management, responsible as well for any changes one might want to make to university space, asked 'Who?' What she actually said was,

> Who, exactly who, is to be included in this accessible classroom? And who is the adjoining special washroom for? You can't accommodate everybody. You've got to draw the line somewhere. Really, think about it, worst case scenario, is your classroom for forty people going to fit forty people in wheelchairs. Your plan needs to include many more details about who, who exactly, is this space for. (AIF Accessible Classroom, Meeting Notes, November, 2007)

I thought that using universal design principles to make a flexible and inclusive classroom space was a sufficient plan for the more than half a million dollars in grant money my department secured in order to build an accessible, state-of-the-art classroom. Universal design principles are oriented to making space more available to more people, or 'making products, communications, and the built environment more usable by as many people as possible' (Center for Universal Design, 2008: http://www.design.ncsu.edu/cud/, accessed July 17, 2008). For the person in charge of space, however, this plan needed to include many more details – but not details about universal design. Instead, the desired details were about the particular people who might come to inhabit this space.

Both the number and type of students were at issue for the space management person. Such a concern is, in part, born of bureaucratically managed educational space. Within the neo-liberal milieu of the early twenty-first century, university students are habitually referred to, or made to represent, a BIU – a Basic Income Unit. Universities receive funding on the basis of these units. For example, in the Province of Ontario, undergraduates are viewed as between one and three BIUs whereas doctoral students count as six. Through various calculations of the number and types of BIUs within, universities receive their funding.

In 2009 in Ontario, universities received less than five thousand dollars of government funding for each BIU – an allocation which universities routinely say is insufficient (OCUFA, 2008: 3). Nonetheless, accounting for students *as* BIUs continues to hold sway throughout many different aspects of university life, including in the discussion of space for an already-funded classroom.

One cost that students represent is connected to space: students take up space, and space (like time) is money in the sense that its allocation and use can be measured through a cost-benefit rationale. But, given that space and time could be understood in a multitude of other ways, configuring the cost of space is tied to making its typical use a known and measurable entity. Typical use presupposes a typical *user* – and this user is the 'student' pictured as an economic unit. The student as a BIU is thus one ordinary way[1] to depict typical use of space and other resources in the university environment. BIUs are a way of imaging how to address almost any decision in university life, ranging from the design of programs, degree requirements, and course provisions, to how to spend time, how to allocate space – or even how to imagine who should and should not take up space. Such accounting procedures resist addressing interests that are not figured strictly in cost-benefit terms, such as critical curriculum development, principles of inclusion, or issues of human rights. Instead, such accounting procedures transform educational stuff into a measurable unit based on costs and benefits (this is also how neo-liberalism operates on the organization of health care, emergency preparedness, and social supports). Moreover, people at the university who administer this type of work can and do make decisions on the basis of such calculations.

Into the midst of these calculations – enter disability. Disability joins a discussion about designing a classroom which is *already fully funded*, and funded by a grant secured on the principal of including disability. But, even though disability was not originally a funding issue, it is transformed into one. Disability is something exceptionally variable and in need of measurement – expressed in this example by the phrase 'Really, think about it, worst case scenario, is your classroom for forty people going to fit forty people in wheelchairs.' Forty people in wheelchairs represent more space being taken up and this represents more cost. After all, non-wheelchair users take up less space, and therefore cost less. Even though funding is secured, there is the future use of the room to consider, and in these neo-liberal times that consideration entails a cost-benefit analysis.

If we grant that the spirit of cost-benefit rationality is animating the classroom design exchange, then there are two dominant features that make disability into a 'worst case scenario,' even though disability is the 'funder' of the project. First, forty wheelchair users are imagined as those who will, at some future time, take up more space than forty non-wheelchair-users. (Interestingly enough, forty non-wheelchair-users require chairs, which is a cost that wheelchair users do not present to the university.) Under cost-benefit rationality it is good, or at least normal, to regard students in terms of the future costs of their taking up space. But there is more that is related to the second way that disability is made into a worst case scenario. Disability is disruptive to a taken-for-granted sense of who normally belongs, and, in this particular exchange, disability represents more tasks and diverse calculations for the space management person.

Thus, disruption is also figured as an expense. 'Everybody' needs to be measured. The unit of measurement is not, however, every body but only a mythical, normalized body imagined through the regularity of the student as a BIU. In the face of disability, this cost-benefit rationality is disrupted. The units of analysis, both students and social space, are no longer as easily measured and accounted for since the standard forms of measurement (normal student, normal classroom) are not standard – and, ironically, *never* were such (Gabel, 2005; Graham and Slee, 2008).

One way to make sense of cost-benefit arguments, which erupt with regular frequency in the daily life of the university, is to understand them as the mechanism whereby we convince each other that it is good to measure people and social space – and, more basically, that these things 'are' measurable. It may seem that measuring both the quantity and quality of human existence occurs only in extreme acts of degradation, such as justifying the killing of Tracy Latimer or Terri Schiavo, using disability rates to calculate a country's economic limits and disadvantages (DALY's), or in designing emergency preparedness programs which assume a higher death rate among the 'vulnerable.' But, as this analysis of classroom design is beginning to reveal, measuring the cost of people is a routine part of the organization of the most ordinary aspects of everyday life – such as being in classrooms, entering doorways, turning on computers, and distributing course outlines. More disturbing than the quantification of human life and limb is the social fact that this repetitive, routine practice can remain unquestioned and can continue to produce the differential value of people.

By pointing out the difficulty of including the excluded Other, educational space and bodies are being naturalized as normal and measurable entities (Graham and Slee, 2008). Disability does not fit as a standard BIU configuration of bodies in space, and so it is made into an exceptional unit of cost. Moreover, disability is unimaginable from the point of view of rational choice economic theory, for who would choose disability? Disability must be seen as the exception, not the rule, for the system of BIU's to remain intact. Its inability to fit with the established accounting procedures, which are taken as basic and even natural ways of proceeding, makes it appear *as if* disability cannot fit at all. This rationality grounds the 'sensibility' of discussions regarding designing an accessible classroom with funds already secured for exactly this purpose, beginning with a forceful assertion that 'you can't accommodate everyone.'

Cost-benefit accounting procedures get a little messed up when disability is 'thrown into the mix,' not only because disability exceeds such accounting procedures but also, as Paul Hunt (1998) reminds us, because cost-benefit analysis cannot adequately address the critical condition of life itself – nor can a cost-benefit rationality address how people allocate value in the first place. Nonetheless, when disability is taken as something that basically does not belong, it allows for the management of disability as an exception. Its cost will still need to be calculated and contained, but within a status framed as rare and anomalous.

It is thus a very strange disruption, indeed, to regard disability as key to the plan, as not only a possible participant but a desirable one. Such a conception ends up throwing out all the standard ways of making students into basic units of cost which can be known, planned for, and otherwise managed. That disability becomes a 'worst case scenario' not only reflects prejudice but also reflects how disability is readily imagined as disrupting the clear-cut accounting procedures used to manage space under the neo-liberal rule of late capitalism. Transforming the plurality of the student body into the singular identity of a BIU 'not only diminishes us all, it also makes the world much more flammable' (Sen, 2006: 16). The flammable world is the one that makes lives, and perhaps more and more of them, exceptional costs whose belonging is uncertain and even unnecessary.

Still, the best part of the worst case scenario is that disability provokes thoughts about how the social ordering of space, time, and money, and all the ways these things limit access, are actually tied to how we can and cannot imagine *who* people are, *who* belongs, and how collectives orient to embodiment. Through such questioning, we can access the sense in which economic decisions are *not* based strictly on dollar figure calculations but on taken-for-granted configurations of humanity. My aim is to show that disability is a space where it is possible to gain access to the social and political meaning attributed to being human. I turn now to more fully opening the question of 'who?' as this entails the drawing of lines, or boundaries, around legitimate participation and thus invites our reflection on the constitution of who belongs.

Who Belongs?

Inasmuch as the line between inclusion and exclusion needs to be drawn somewhere, it is sometimes recommended that certain bodies be regarded as out of line with social spaces, since space can be conceived as not for everybody. Thus, 'Who, exactly who, is to be included . . . You can't accommodate everybody. You've got to draw the line somewhere.' The body of concern, the 'worst case scenario,' is the disabled one, signified, in this case, by wheelchair use. It is important to understand that the phrase 'You can't accommodate everybody,' while often spoken, is not unquestionable truth endowed with the power of nature. 'You can't accommodate everybody' is a way of bringing bodies and space to a consciousness where some bodies are made and regarded as 'naturally' a problem for some spaces.

Perceiving bodies as out of line with social space is a more common everyday activity than it may, at first, seem. For example, at the University of Toronto Office of Space Management website, classroom space is depicted in relation to campus location, seating allocation, multi-media technological resource availability, and whether or not the classroom is regarded as wheelchair accessible (http://www.osm.utoronto.ca/, accessed May 8, 2009). It is important to note that wheelchair access is the only form of access delineated, and whether or not the 'multi-media' resource is accessible to blind, D/deaf, or learning disabled people is not mentioned. The question, 'Wheelchair Accessible?' is answered by highlighting either a 'Yes' box or a 'No' box. In relation to disability and access, this 'yes or no' is the basic information regarding classroom space that is ordinarily expected from universities today. It is only through the taken-for-granted sense that bodies can be regarded as 'naturally' out of line with social space that so few details regarding the space of the university can serve as an ordinary way to depict classroom accessibility. Assuming that a check in the yes box means that the classroom is accessible to wheelchair users does not mean these students can use the classroom. For example, the building that contains the classroom may not be accessible; the route to the classroom may present a barrier to wheelchair users; or there may be no accessible bathroom in the vicinity of the accessible classroom, and so forth. These examples are not hypothetical; such conditions do exist on university campuses that have not begun to imagine questions of access in more collective, more rigorous, and less individualized ways. It is not hallways, offices, washrooms, and so on that are being evaluated as in or out of line with bodies; instead, questions of access are located on the bodies themselves. Therefore, bodies are noticed as either in or out of line with space. A 'Yes/ No' relation to classroom evaluation functions only insofar as space is conceived of as relatively stable and hospitable.

What, then, does listing classrooms as 'Wheelchair Accessible? Yes/ No' do, even if it does not serve as adequate access information? This practice shows the ordinariness of the daily act of regarding bodies as out of line with social space. Such organized practices also make a lack of accommodation and various exclusions not noticeable – at least, not ordinarily. Such information demonstrates that an ordinary way of noticing exclusion, for example, is restricted to accessibility to wheelchair use.

The echoes of 'You can't accommodate everybody' are also found in the more formal or legal approach to disability, which speaks of disability through the language of 'reasonable accommodation.' An accommodation is not regarded as reasonable if it costs an organization too much, with costs being measured primarily in terms of money and safety. Human rights legislation refers to this excess cost of accommodation as 'undue hardship.' Of course, the act of safe economic reasoning is accomplished somewhere, and that somewhere is usually within the space of unexamined conceptions of the status quo. That all faculty and staff members should, for example, move the coat trees from behind their office doors so as to enable the door to open fully, thereby allowing people with mobility devices to enter, is a reasonable accommodation – it costs neither time nor money and may even enhance safety. That all faculty members should receive an automated door opener is another story. That people do or do not consider their offices in relation to access issues is yet another one. It is this latter story with which I am most concerned. What is interesting about stories of office doors that cannot open fully is that they tell us that we do not raise the question of 'who belongs?' even as we answer it, thus we may not be asking, 'Who do we need to be when we are in our space?' This non-questioning is as important an access issue as is the consideration of cost-benefit calculative processes behind many 'reasonable' accommodation deliberations (Prince, 2009: 202).

How people talk about matters of access or accommodation has something to teach us regarding who we are, and this is not just because such talk reveals a bureaucratic milieu, an economic rationale, or a legalistic mindset. Matters of access and accommodation rely on, and constitute, conceptions of who belongs, and this remains true whether coat trees are moved or not – or whether classrooms are redesigned or not. Legalistic bureaucratic manoeuvres establish normalcy through an 'unsaying; an absence of descriptions' (Graham and Slee, 2008: 287) by drawing lines around the idea that it is good to have an operating sense of types of people who are beyond inclusion. A sense of the normal participant, not to mention normalcy itself, is achieved by imagining, discussing, and perhaps even describing the type who is outside normalcy while maintaining an illusory sense that exclusion is an act of nature and not a social act. Inasmuch as a 'naturally excluded' type is secured, more specific lines of exclusion can be drawn. Thus, any answer to the question, 'Who, who exactly is the classroom for?' is as much a depiction of who might be excluded as it is of who might be included. Moreover, answering the question of who space is for makes the drawing of such lines seem natural and ordinary. Lines are, in other words, *always* being drawn by the way in which access is discussed.

The question of 'who?' can achieve many things and produce radically different divisions, and this is provocative. Who are you? Who are you to me? Who's who around here? Who should we invite? And, most provocatively: Who do we need to exclude? Since it stands to reason that we all need to draw the line somewhere – 'You can't accommodate everybody.' 'Who?' is a question that gives shape to a particular form of consciousness of access. For example, access can be understood as limited 'because' bodies have different ways of being that are neither expected nor welcomed, and this transforms an imagined group of wheelchair users into a 'worst case scenario.' What might individual or collective imaginative relations to the excludable other have to say about who we are? How is it that the question of 'who,' when directed at disability, so poignantly brings to the fore the uncertainty of belonging? Who are we – 'we' in the contemporary Western university systems – such that 'who?' questions can become such efficacious ways of producing exclusionary practices?

Who Is Drawing Lines?

It is difficult, perhaps impossible, to ask a 'who?' question that does not draw lines; any answer to 'who?' relies on and makes distinctions. Consider, for example:

> Who, me? I am a university professor doing disability studies in the Department of Sociology and Equity Studies at OISE in Toronto.
>
> Who, me? I am a white, middle-class woman who grew up in Calgary.
>
> Who, me? Oh, about five days a week I go for a workout usually right after I write for a bit in the morning.
>
> Who, me? I am dyslexic; my partner is blind; we are part of a growing group of scholars who argue that we need to think more about social space and the meaning of embodiment in everyday life.
>
> Who, me? I am someone who appears to the space management person as one who undoubtedly belongs in the university environment, but also as one who can and should make plans about who does not.

Every answer to 'who?' moves immediately into the identification of a 'what?' Wondering about the difficulty of speaking directly about who people are, Hannah Arendt (1958: 181) says,

> The moment we want to say *who* somebody is, our very vocabulary leads us astray into saying *what* he [*sic*] is; we get entangled in a description of qualities he necessarily shares with others like him; we begin to describe a type or a 'character'. . .

In finding things to say *about* who one is, we offer a sense of a character's status or social location, or we offer a depiction of pursuing this activity or that, or we describe the beliefs, privileges, and powers exercised by the person. We offer versions or qualities of a type – identity placeholders shared by many other people but nonetheless put to use to answer a particular 'who?' question. Saying what someone is or does serves to gesture towards, or indirectly represent, who they are. Who, then, lies partially revealed in what I identify, be it working out, writing, teaching, dyslexia, relations to disability, scholarship, or activism. Similarly, there is a partially revealed who that lies in the act of identifying a group of wheelchair users as a worst case scenario, just as there is a partially revealed who in the act of using disability funds to build a 'special' university classroom.

Even though it is impossible to speak directly about who without moving towards saying what someone does, feels, thinks, or appears like, there are still things to learn from the common activity of asking 'who?' Responding to the space management person's comment about the necessity of excluding some people, I said,

> Yes, maybe forty people using wheelchairs, maybe some with scooters, some with power chairs, others with manual chairs, some might have an attendant or a service dog, others might also be blind or deaf or what have you – we could have an international conference and invite disabled people from around the world – it's very exciting that this space could accommodate so many!

Still, whether regarded as the worst case scenario or the best case scenario, both rely on a taken-for-granted understanding of who typically or normally is imagined as a legitimate participant and give rise to differing images of who belongs. No one is saying, 'Oh yes, people with two legs, two arms, two eyes, and ears all in ordinary working order – it's all very exciting.' Bureaucratic life relies upon actual bodies disappearing, becoming illusory background figures on the foreground of bureaucratic management (Ferguson and Titchkosky, 2008; Hughes and Paterson, 1997). It is in this way that bodies become mere scenarios. Giving answers to the 'who?' question does the work of making distinctions – this means that everyone already *is* drawing the line somewhere. There is always some sense of a who that resides in our act of making distinctions regarding what we and others do, say, think, and feel.

'Who?' is a question of knowledge tied to the power of division, since to know something of who you are dealing with is to make distinctions, to sort, and to draw lines. Likewise, to know places and their dividing lines is also to sort out and know who's who. Who we are taken to be and who we are positioned with also provide different forms of the power of sorting. The question, 'Who, who exactly is to be included?' draws on a powerfully provocative form of sorting. Those who 'we' can't, won't, or don't imagine as potential participants are those who remain excludable, even as a more inclusive version of who belongs is developed. In this way, assertions of inclusion help to normalize conceptions of those who are *essentially excludable*. Essentially excludable – this is a dominant conception of disability that operates in everyday life.

Whether forty people who use wheelchairs do or do not come to use the accessible classroom is not the point. The point is that by asking who will potentially be present, we are re-establishing and reaffirming norms regarding the ordinary shape of participation – the shape of the person and the shape of the space. Participation is shaped by the imagined shape of the participants and of the space of participation. Another shape that participation takes is one that is emboldened to draw lines around the boundaries of participation itself. Participation in the form of shaping participation is a powerful irony which is important to acknowledge if this shape is ever to change.

Disability, even as essentially excludable, is still included on a case-by-case – that is, individual – basis. Individuals and their individualized special needs, imagined as possibly present in individual classrooms, are who and what typically receive accommodative attention in universities today. Most accommodation and access procedures draw clear lines between the individual and the environment. This requires accommodation to be thought of as a decontextualized, individual matter that follows some individual people with disabilities – individual transportability of accommodative measures. When inclusive measures are perceived as necessarily following individual disabled people, belonging takes shape as personal adjustment. If accommodative measures are perceived as necessarily wrapped up in the organization of space and activities, then belonging will need to be imagined as a complex form of interrelatedness between people and where they find themselves. In short, there are many different ways to order belonging.

It is impossible for any answer to 'who are you?' not to reveal something about the context of social relations within which the question is asked, and through which a sense of who we are is indirectly expressed. It is impossible to answer definitively who public space is for, since it can never really be known who might show up – the excluded, the unimagined, or the unwelcomed do show up from time to time (Michalko and Titchkosky, 2001). Space is realigned despite anyone's best or worst intentions. When the unexpected show up in university life, we can learn something about the substance of collective and individual versions of 'who's who.'

The question is not only who gets in and who is left out; it is also the types of people imagined as in and the types of people imagined as out. The question is also who a community becomes as it makes room, in particular ways, for its traditionally excluded others. There are ways of including forty wheelchair users that might only affirm a taken-for-granted sense of disability as nothing but a worst case scenario. That social space and subjectivity are interwoven and mutually constitutive is no mere abstraction – this is how we make the meaning of people. This means that access to space is intimately tied with the structures of subjectivity. Yet Western cultures typically and routinely bring access to attention as though it is merely a substance to be measured for its presence or absence, as exemplified by the 'yes/no' check box found on university website descriptions of classrooms. There are, then, few ways available to access access as it forms our consciousness of the relation between people and spaces.

The relation between spaces, who we are, and who we might become represents a space for questioning the meaning of disability, non-disability, and their embodied interrelation. As a way to illustrate this, I turn to a narrative account of arriving at my new university. Relying on my own experience of dyslexia as I began work at the University of Toronto, I provide a stage for exploring how we imagine legitimate participation. I tell this story to bring to the fore the need to consider the shifting lines and hierarchies of inclusion as these relate to questions of knowledge production.

A Moving Story: Who Are You?

Summer, 2006, and I've arrived! I've just arrived in Toronto. I am their new hire. I am their new professor of disability studies at the Ontario Institute for Studies in Education of the University of Toronto. What a long name, but most people simply say OISE/UT. And I have arrived with stuff, almost ten years of stuff from being a professor elsewhere. With any big life move there is so much to do, so much to learn, and, of course, there is stuff, so much stuff. I have plenty of it to sort out, to set up, including furniture and books, boxes of them; boxes and boxes of books. Coming from Antigonish, Nova Scotia, and while many days late, the movers and all this stuff finally pull into the big T.O.

First, it's apartment stuff. It is delivered. And with this comes the necessity to account for all the boxes. 'Here's the bingo sheet,' says one of the movers. 'Look, the guys are going to come in and call out the numbers – you check them off.' And it starts. One of the three movers comes into our apartment, carrying a box, and calls out, '136.'

I am guessing now that there is a number on every box. Okay, find the number on the long sheet of lists of numbers and check it off – that's all.

'Check,' I say.

'178.'

'. . . check.'

'131.'

'157,' says another.

'131. Did you get 131?'

'3 . . . no, 1. What?' I ask.

Rod, my partner who is blind, helps me out. He starts memorizing the streams of numbers that keep bouncing in the door and around the apartment and this gives me a bit more time to find them on the sheet and check them off. Still, I feel both rushed and mistaken . . . I am mixing up their order, looking for numbers on the bingo sheet, looking for 301 instead of 103. Remember. The high numbers are not even on the bingo sheet. Remember?

Rod repeats.

I get it.

Then, we get busy and catch another number.

I think I see a moving guy putting book's on our bookshelves with the spines hidden to the back. That can't be! But it hardly matters now since it seems that I have got all the numbers. The apartment stuff is in. This part of the move – all done.

Same guys, same truck, but now my office stuff will be delivered at OISE/UT, 252 Bloor Street West. My new office is on the top floor, the twelfth floor, my office in the department of Sociology and Equity Studies in Education. Most people call it SESE, sometimes said 'sessy.' Even while I have been without my books for some time now, I have had a great view from my office in SESE. But I need to meet up with the movers first, through the bowels of the building. I am to meet the movers at the OISE delivery doors, in the basement . . . no, no, the 'Concourse.' I am to go to the Concourse and get a special elevator key which I will turn in a special spot in the elevator key pad after we meet at another elevator, the freight elevator, where all deliveries must arrive. I know all this because I have been told by the people who work in the receiving office. Moreover, I have been practising what I was told.

Three times prior to moving day, I went down to the Concourse level and spoke to the two women who work in receiving, either one of whom would be here today, moving day, to hand over the special key. On each visit, I ask many questions. Each time, I practise the new directions, memorize the look of the hallways in relation to the elevators,

I imagine turning the special key in the correct direction. The women who work there introduce me to the frightful freight elevator door that opens up and down with a metallic slam and could, they say, 'take your arm off!'

I acquaint myself with all of this because I want to get it straight; I want to make at least this part of the move, the part where I have some control, smooth – hassle free. Correct.

I know that as I enter the main front doors of OISE, the movers are parking their massive truck at its delivery or receiving entrance. I am simply hoping that my practise does make perfect. I walk into OISE, hop on an elevator, travel down to the Concourse, pull open the receiving office door, get the key, back out the door, into the hall and off I go. Correct?

Things don't look quite the same. I am trying to figure it out. I need to figure out where to go to find the freight elevator. Is this key for the freight elevator or for the elevator that goes up to the twelfth floor? I can't seem to figure out how to get back out of the bowels of the building to where the movers are waiting for me. Then, I am back in the place from where I got the key. I have the key, could I also now have her help?

But she can't. The woman behind the counter says that it's the other woman's lunch hour, so she can't leave. I can understand that. I go back to try to find my way to the freight elevator. Out the door again, down the hallway, past the yellow lockers . . . but where is it? This hallway, with its mass of yellow lockers, is confusing. Or am I mistaken again? I think the movers will know what to do with the elevator key, so I will stop worrying about that, but I can't find the movers. And if I find the freight elevator, do I go up or do I go down to meet them? Maybe the elevator buttons will make that clear. Why can't I find the elevator? Surely anyone can find an elevator. What if I don't meet up with the movers, will they just leave the stuff at receiving? I guess I could move the books myself. But how does a freight elevator just vanish; am I on the wrong floor, is this the wrong hallway?

Something is wrong.

I go back to the woman. I want to keep her in sight since I know that she knows where everything is. She knows where the elevator is and how to use it; she knows how to get to ground level, or delivery level, Concourse level, or whatever level I am supposed to be on. I know she knows where the movers are, and clearly, she knows where she is. I do not.

Okay, it is clear, I get it. I don't know where I am and I don't know what to do and I don't know how to put it straight. And, I don't like it. I hate it! And then I hate that I hate it.

'Please,' I say to her, and tears begin to well up. Then I say it. Maybe my tears might have been enough to release her from her lunchtime work obligations, but I still feel compelled to say something. After all, she deserves an explanation for why I, a most friendly and inquisitive professor who has been coming by for a visit every day, is now stuck and in tears. 'Please, come help me, I am dyslexic and I'm lost.'

And, she does.

Rethinking the Stories of Who

The woman from receiving did, in fact, help me; I did get my stuff; my books are all set up; and many people today agree that I have a nice office with a good view. But my point is not that all's well that ends well. Nor is the point that I could have done things differently, disclosed or self-identified much earlier, and saved myself and the women in receiving some grief, even though this is possibly true. Improving access for ourselves and for others is certainly part of the story, but it is not the whole of it, nor is it the end of it. That this articulation of who I take myself to be – dyslexic – could hold an almost magical power to secure help is something to think about. My story, for example, gives us various entrées to the question of 'who?' Who is expected in the university environment? Who is disabled in this story? What do we expect from who we depict as being disabled? We can access all these questions since any story is simultaneously a reflection of the culture upon which the story relies for its telling and into which it is told.

First, consider the end point – 'Please, come help me, I am dyslexic and I'm lost.' A self in need of help articulated as a 'lost self' serves to resolve the dilemma in this story. Not only is the claim to dyslexia aiming to secure help, it is also aiming to secure sheer sensibility. The story makes the assumption that dyslexia is a way to narrate and make sensible how and why someone is lost in a somewhat familiar environment. The phrase, 'Please, come help me, I am dyslexic and . . .' does more than provide an explanation for tears and is more than the act of self-identification. The words 'I am dyslexic' make the problem of being lost in, and uncertain about, the normative order of the environment appear as a 'particular' type of problem – a personal problem. 'Dyslexia' is also assumed to make sense of, or even announce, a person's transition from friendly-privileged-white-woman to a lost individual requiring assistance. It propels me from a general category – professor – to a more particular identity category – professor moving books who is having difficulty doing so, a professor who needs help. While 'privileged white woman' surely helps to secure this assistance, the utterance 'I am dyslexic and I'm lost' achieves 'disability' as the grounds for the request for help and makes the need for help appear sensible and necessary. The answer to the question 'Who is disabled?' becomes 'Someone who needs and, simultaneously, deserves help.' This story works insofar as the definition of disability as a need for help is operative for me and for the woman from receiving. Who we are when we access conceptions of disability are representatives of a culture who have both received and reproduced the sensibility of disability in particular ways.

Still, it is not that the workplace expects dyslexic professors, or any other sort of disability, to show up. What members of a workplace can expect is that there might be some differences to which it may be reasonable to respond. All people, under contemporary conditions, need help with moving; only some people need certain forms of help, such as finding elevators or remembering numbers. Embodied difference in my story is not the rule, it is the exception. Accommodative workplace procedures or demands can reaccomplish disability as an exceptional need for help, rightly deserved. And such procedures would help by containing the request in the shape of an 'individual need,' almost disconnected from environmental organization and normative demands. Disability, in my story, is also a category that references a version of *just enough*. Disability signifies something that is just enough unlike others so as to secure a unique version of help, and just enough like others to be recognized as a valid form of participation. The other in regard to which disability is positioned as just enough is, of course, the order of normalcy. All people receive help from others. Yet some people, and only some, appear as those who are in need of help. What remains is the sense that disability is some kind of disqualification from the demands of normalcy that must seek some form of reconciliation with those same demands.

Today, this reconciliation takes one dominant form, which my story participates in reproducing. My story joins forces with most governments around the globe by adhering to, and perpetuating an understanding of, disability as an 'inability to perform an activity in the manner or within the range considered normal for a human being' because of a 'loss or abnormality of a psychological, or anatomical structure or function' (WHO, 1980). This version of disability makes an appearance in my story far before its conclusion. Let us reconsider, for example, that I narrate the following. 'Rod, my partner who is blind, helps me out. He starts memorizing the streams of numbers that keep bouncing in the door and around the apartment and this gives me a bit more time to find them on the sheet and check them off.' Partners who help partners in the midst of major life events are part of my taken-for-granted assumption of how things work. But instead of doing it for me or doing it along with me, Rod's help is beside me, and my story makes this a signifier of disability. This division of labour is taken by me as unique enough to warrant the explanation, 'Rod, my partner *who is blind*, helps me out' with his memory. Once again, my story of seeking access provides all who read it access to disability as, among other things, an inability to perform the activities of daily living in a way considered normal for a human being. Still, the question remains, How does access act as a form of consciousness regarding who people are? So, there is still more to access from this access story.

Theorizing as Boundary Crossing

'Dyslexia' often does the work of making sense of all sorts of problems, anomalies, or boundary crossings. Why is the newcomer, who has been told what to do, not doing what she was told? Why is she asking for personal guidance when others need only verbal directions? Why is a friendly person now crying? How is it that a professor who has been told three times now where the elevator is, and what the routine is, cannot use what she knows to do what she wishes? How is it that someone could be lost in plain sight? 'Dyslexia' is the device I use, and invite the woman to use, in order for all this to make sense. An answer to the question 'who?' is used to make sense of what I am and am not doing; and it is used to make sense of where the lines are usually drawn regarding what people usually do. Moreover, what I am – dyslexic – has something to say about who is and is not expected by this environment.

The woman in the receiving office may have had no prior knowledge of dyslexia, nor its reference to mix-ups beyond words; mix-ups in logical sequences and in following directions, or of not getting matters of space and time straight and normal 'like everyone else.' But such detailed knowledge is not necessary. All that is necessary is that dyslexia signifies *disability* and thus draws on its common, taken-for-granted cultural meaning: this culture insists that disability is a problem possessed by individuals, found in individuals, unrelated to the normative order of the environment or social space, and is best dealt with by individual accommodative or rehabilitative procedures – in short, by helping. The environment does not have a problem, I do. The claim to 'dyslexia' as the reason for why I am not doing what I wish to do individualizes the problem while normalizing the current state of affairs of the university environment. I got help, but my passing teardrop most likely did not leave a dent on the environment.

While parts of the environment remain untouched, the claim of dyslexia frees us both from 'normal role obligations' – she can now imagine leaving her desk; I can now get access to the ability to accomplish my tasks of daily living. 'Please, come help me, I am dyslexic and I'm lost' makes manifest an invisible issue, a state of exception, by prescribing ways of conceiving of dealing with me. Dyslexia appears, as it helps me to perform a retelling of a part of my past, as a way of securing a more certain future – namely, some help. And, in the context of my white, middle-class, professorial privilege, the words did indeed function this way. I did get help. This means that 'I am dyslexic' functions as a sense-making device both for me and for those who are dealing with me. From this we can learn that the words of a culture are a doing of that culture. But what are these disability words doing?

'Disability,' in the stories in this chapter, serves as a sense-making device for unexpected departures from the routine order of institutional life. This holds true as much in my individual story of arriving at my place of work as it does in the planning of a state-of-the-art classroom that is supposed to be fully accessible. Disability is a way to make disruptions to the normative order sensible, and it does so even for orders steeped in the norm of disruption itself, such as moving; classroom design; and any other space/time issue. Disability does this sense-making work insofar as it signifies that the trouble a person seems to be having within the normal, routine orders is itself caused by a 'problem,' not of order but of individuals. Individuals have disabilities and rarely do we think of the environment as disabling, nor do we think of disability as something more than a problem, exceeding a need for containment, elimination, or solution.

'Disability' can be used to make sense of so much only insofar as we live in a culture that understands the primary meaning of disability to be 'individual-with-problem,' as well as an exception to the rule of normal expectations. I reproduced this meaning, relied upon on it, and, unlike over 33 per cent of other Canadians with Disabilities (between

3.6 and 4.2 million people), I got the help that I needed (Canada, 2004, 2002; HRDC, 2006). Taking disability as an embodied individual issue, and not as a complex set of meanings located in cultural processes, is a barrier to accessing a collective desire to form new relations between who people are and where they find themselves.

We need a more complex story and we need to complicate the stories that we already have. We need stories that will engage with the set of meanings of disability located in cultural processes; this means understanding that we are never alone in our bodies. Disability and the questions of access are not restricted to the question of identifying individuals with a problem, since even the most individualized disability experience is fully enmeshed in cultural representations of disability. It is, therefore, necessary to move from the question of 'who?' to the question of 'what?' What is disability? What do people, including disabled people, say disability is? What do representations of disability have to do with who disabled people are?

3 'What?': Representing Disability

This chapter addresses the question of 'what?'[1] In particular, what images of disability do we typically find within the university environment and what are we doing when we represent disability in this way or that? By images of disability, I mean *any* appearance of disability, since any such appearance is generated through our collective acts of interpretation. The question, then, becomes, *'what* are we doing when we represent disability in the ways that we do?' It is important that we begin with the understanding that, within the university context, we represent disability within a bureaucratized version of conducting human affairs. This social context generates its own ordinary, everyday ways of representing disability. We can now ask, 'What have we made disability to be?'

I consider ordinary representations of disability as found in everyday linguistic expressions and symbols. In the previous chapter, I examined the all-too-certain depiction of disability as a particular person who is in need of help. As dominant as this depiction is, it should also be clear that disability is more and other than an individual matter. Just as '[w]e must always mean more and other than we mean to say/write' (Smith, 1999a: 103), we must always mean more and other than what we mean when we do. One way to begin to imagine this 'more than' is to reflectively engage the dominant representations of disability that necessarily make embodied life 'less than' it is.

To glean something more from these myriad disability representations, we need to approach them with questions rather than with certainty. One way of pursuing the necessity of opening that which is typically taken for granted, and thus certain, is to interrogate ordinary representations of disability. What do people receive access to in the act of noticing disability in the everyday life of the university environment, especially when what is noticed is something other than an individual disabled person? A further issue worthy of examination is that there is a gap between the common act of regarding who disabled people are as individuals, with individual needs, who may or may not belong; and the collective ways that disability is sometimes represented as a potential participant through legislation and signs of access.

Signs of access, for example, are strewn throughout the University of Toronto campus. But what is disability such that it needs this access signage? These questions suggest that there is more to these signs than the presence of disability. There is a version of normal disability depiction in the everyday use of these signs, and these versions act to reproduce the power of normalcy. One power of normalcy lies in its ability to actualize both its inclusions and exclusions as though they are ordained by nature. Regarded as natural, concepts of normalcy organize the shape of daily life even while closing down the sense that things could or should be otherwise. This chapter will demonstrate the necessary interpretive method of a restless reflexive return to the connections between images of disability – any depiction of *what* we think disability is – and the reproduction of that which counts as normal. By theorizing ways that disability representations appear in everyday life we can *create* a livelier, provocative, and perhaps deliberately different image, an alter-image of disability. The art of theorizing is at work when the matter of normalcy is transformed from a power, against which disability is usually contrasted and controlled, into a place of wonder. This chapter, then, seeks to develop an orientation to what disability is depicted to be in order to question the culture from which these depictions arise.

The Appearances of Disability

Disability makes an appearance as, and in, many different images. We imagine disability in a variety of ways, and when we notice it, we imagine that the image we notice is, indeed, disability.[2] So, let us begin where all disability does: in imagination, in the imaginary act of representing disability. Far from being an individual act, imagining disability is a collective one. Imagination is social – we create images together. Imagination is located in the midst of people, a collective, influenced by and influencing the cultural understandings of all. The concept of imagination reflects the language base (Ricoeur, 1978: 148) or intersubjectivity (Smith, 1999a: 98) of interpretation, the stuff of life.

Understanding this 'stuff' means theorizing how the subject of disability appears in images enmeshed in cultural understandings of what disability is imagined to be.

Not all cultures and not all times have lived with the term 'disability.' The various historically rooted ways to refer to *types* of bodily differences also change from place to place and from time to time (Davis, 1995; Ingstad and Whyte, 1995; Schweik, 2009; Stiker, 1999). The marginalization of disability is also historically rooted and disabled people have not always faced rates of unemployment, underemployment, and poverty two and three times higher than the currently non-disabled (Canada, 2004). Disability is a term that conceptually organizes people into categories whose characteristics are measured and then depicted in government and educational texts. These different appearances of disability mean that from school to home to government, from lover to stranger, to friend – in all locales we represent disability differently depending upon where we find ourselves. As Susan Schweik (2009: 11) says, disability can be regarded as a political process, an event, 'broadly construed.' Thus, when we address the question of what is disability, the first image we need to address is the *term itself.*

Disability appears as we speak of it, represent it. Disability appears in and through the Western(izing) expression 'person with a disability.' The language in 'people with disabilities' is a way to give disability an image. It is also hegemonic in scope. Governments around the globe; the World Health Organization; news media; university disability services offices; most textbooks and course outlines – all these institutions use person-first language and this language has become the dominant linguistic way to represent disability. Person-first language finds its historical roots in Western bureaucratic culture and this 'proper institutional speech' of disability is also the culture's way of shaping a 'proper speaker.'

That we can shape ourselves as proper speakers by speaking of disability as a condition *attached* to a person makes manifest a particular image of what disability is – namely, an impairment condition that comes along with people. The proper speaker is one who does not collapse the difference between person and disability. Disability appears and in so doing ties people to conceptions of legitimacy. Saying, for example, 'disabled people' is not a dominant way of referring to or representing disability today. When Western(ized) people act as legitimate speakers, people-first language schemes are used. This ubiquitous cultural demand to separate disability and personhood remains legitimate except in emergencies, or potential emergencies. In the aftermath of disasters or epidemic preparedness programs, disability is collapsed into the category of 'vulnerable' (e.g., Dowd, 2005). The World Health Organization understands 'vulnerable' to include a 'pre-existing medical condition,' a condition they equate with disability. The category 'vulnerable medical condition' communicates the understanding that something is threatening the continuing possibility of life for some people, and that this threat is not the emergency situation itself. What is threatening life is, of course, disability, understood as a threatening condition that makes people vulnerable. Disability is referred to as an addition, one of vulnerability, to the all-powerful and normal conception of 'person.' People just happen to have a disability attached to them (even though it haunts, in a much more complex way, the accounts of some people's deaths during times of upheaval, such as emergencies).

Disability has appeared in other ways as well. The Government of Canada and thus universities have, for example, variously referred to disabled people as the incapacitated, the disabled, the handicapped, handicap people, the vulnerable, people with special needs, people with challenges. And now these representations of disability have all but disappeared in favour of disability as 'people with disabilities.' While there are some in the disability rights movement who insist that there is a good politics and pride in calling ourselves 'disabled people' (Barnes, 1998; Barton et al., 2002; Michalko, 2002; Overboe, 1999; Oliver, 1990), this is a different image of disability that has yet to gain influence in daily life.

Whether we are called people with disabilities, disabled people, the vulnerable, or something else – whatever the expressions used – categorizing embodied existence cannot be avoided. But categorizing embodied existence can also be theorized and represented differently. And so, there is more . . .

Shifting Images of Disability

Disability appears through worries about how to refer to disability. Shifting names – vulnerable, exceptional, special, and disabled – sometimes strike people as simply scary and elicit the cry, 'Political Correctness! What am I to do? What should I say? What do you/they want me to say?' This is reminiscent of the fable of Chicken Little, who exclaims that the sky is falling – however, in this case, 'The names are changing, the names are changing! There are so many names.' Even though what disability is can be a representation of our fear, fear is not necessarily disability. The worry of expressing disability incorrectly can be read as an acknowledgment of the fact that the world, its images, and its people are in flux and could be otherwise. Disability, too, could be otherwise and we can worry that we might say it differently and thus address a different reality, one which is devalued by our expression.

Worries about referring to disability demonstrate that we orient to the world as an interpretive reality – and suggest, too, that there can be other emotions that exist alongside fear, such as joy. There may be grounds for joy in these shifting names of disability since they indicate a potential shift in images and thus a move away from one totalizing way of imagining disability. Name shifts can be read as the knowledge that all of us have something to do with disability, since it begins where we begin: in imagination. Disability makes an appearance through a collective's image of it, thus through a collective's orientation to the images of disability that it creates. And, as I have said, the dominant image of disability today is the one represented in people-first language. What orientation might we hold to this rather singularly monolithic representation of disability we have created?

Through people-first language, disability – and people identified as disabled – is made to serve as part of a labelling process that privileges personhood. Moreover, 'people with disabilities' (PWD) is a label that gives its bearer access to a sense of personhood as primary and disability as secondary. Between the one who uses the label and the one to whom the label refers, even if they are the same person, there resides a culture which displays a particular imaginative relation to embodiment. Disability represented in person-first language reveals a collective's attempt to value not disability, but the person who happens to have it; it is to say that 'you, too,' are a person even though your disability diminishes your value as a person. By privileging person over disability the hope is that an already diminished category of disability will be further devalued.

The desire to shore up a firm separation between people and disability, by privileging the former and diminishing the latter, points to an image of disability as a kind of danger. The danger is that disability could be mistaken for the person and the person reduced to their condition, as in the asthmatic, the blind, the paraplegic, the mentally impaired, and the disabled. If people are rendered as their condition, the danger is that the privileges and duties of personhood might simply disappear.[3] One way to address this danger is remove disability by putting distance between people and the danger. The depiction of disability as dangerous, however, remains naturalized.

Whether or not the distancing achieved through person-first language will resolve the problem of disability being taken as dangerous is an open question. Still, people-first language does reveal a particular way of imagining disability. It imagines disability, first and foremost, as possessing the power to diminish people; it does not regard disability as a proper or expected aspect of personhood, but instead as a danger to personhood. The corollary is that disability has no power to enhance human life. Disability is not personhood, but it is imagined as having a negative effect on personhood and the hope is that this negativity can be minimized. It is almost superfluous to say that this language does not understand disability as a space from which the meaning of humanity can be explored, but person-first language does recommend caution. We should be cautious in our approach to disability since it is dangerous, after all. We should cautiously move disability to the rear and move personhood to the front with the hope of removing, or at least minimizing, the danger that disability is.

This most common and global image of disability organizes and controls the difference that disability is. Fundamentally, then, person-first language represents disability as a problem and imagines its solution as removing disability to the rear of social identity. The work of controlling the difference of disability is, as Rod Michalko (2002) demonstrates, an ongoing contemporary project. Michalko shows how disability is constituted as a difference that ought not make a difference, but also that this is still an act of social constitution since disability is never found in the body alone. Disability resides between people, in imaginative relations. Even in person-first language, disability is still made to appear through our collective imagination. What is disability, then? Disability is an imagined object; it is made present always as an interpretive act. This means disability can always be read as a promise since it will exceed the confines of any singular rendering.

Re-Imagining Disability

Let us begin again . . . in imagination. When we imagine disability, we create an image. We may choose to imagine a wheelchair, a missing limb, blindness, or a white cane; a professional sign language interpreter; a roomful of activists, artists, or scholars; perhaps a set of stairs, an absent chair; a poorly designed classroom, or parking nowhere to be found.

We may imagine disability through a character in a Heidi Janz short story or a Lynn Manning play; or through an Eli Clare poem; an Eliza Chandler video; a Sunny Taylor painting.[4] We also imagine disability in university life. On most campuses today, disability is imagined as a deficit and is acted upon as such. As deficit, disability is addressed through technology design, medical research, special education, physical and occupational therapy, social work, economics, law, and many other professional orientations to deficit. Disability is used metaphorically to represent evil or pathetic characters in literature and religion; it is also used in contemporary representations of extraordinary events or occurrences – 'the traffic is crazy,' 'that was a lame party,' 'she turned a deaf ear,' 'the economy is crippled,' 'the subway system is disabled.' These are just some of the many ways of imagining disability.

In inviting ourselves to imagine disability we are simultaneously given access to culture; we never imagine disability in a social vacuum, but instead perceive it through our cultural assumptions. While there is no one correct representation of disability, there are typical representations of embodied difference that *count* as disability in Westernized cultures. These cultures make use of disability to devalue the lives of other marginalized people. For example, the social process of racialization often includes disability as a descriptive device to devalue people and remove any social conditions as the genesis of poverty, oppression, and marginalization.

Imagining disability is, more often than not, imagining wheelchair use. We can re-imagine disability not merely as a physical – thus visible – entity, but as a different way of being-in-the-world, as a different way of perceiving and accessing that world. Another imaginative turn is revealed here; a subject split and reconnected to her own ways of perceiving; a subject using a disability to represent herself; a subject claiming disability as a subjectivity; perhaps imagining a subject herself in the category of disability.

Imagination includes all the stuff of culture, its norms, and its assumptions within which and through which our embodied differences are made to appear. Disability does, indeed, come to us replete with imaginative meanings that culture has already put there and this is how disability works to sort and govern people. For example, things do happen to dyslexics that do not happen to others. Some differences do make an appearance through practices of reading, mass literacy programs, the prevalence of print, patterned and rule-driven modes of comportment, and the like. It is these cultural practices and assumptions that we get access to and we need to return to them as a way to reflect on the relations we establish to representations of disability.

But fear rises yet again, and it rises in a twist of the 'what' question – 'What if?' What if our belief in the clear certainty of disability as *in* those bodies – those bodies over there, the ones that have 'gone wrong' – what if disability isn't so certain and isn't so distant? What if it isn't over there and singularly confined to those, over there, with problems? What if, like breath itself, we share in disability's appearance? What if my dyslexia is neither in me only nor mine alone?

Saying that we share in disability is not the same as saying that 'everyone is disabled' in some way. In fact, this cliché may distance disability. Nor am I reiterating the fact that we all will be disabled if we live long enough. Instead, I am referring to a kind of sharing that recognizes that everyone participates in making what is noticed and imagined as disability. Thus, disability is an interpretive act that 'enacts or produces that which it names' (Butler, 1993: 13). And yet there are so few invitations to participate in the art of welcoming, and wondering about, the ambiguity that resides in the fact that we are always part of the meaning of others, including disabled others. This disabled other can reside in the disabled self as well. By returning to how we commonly speak of disability, we find the invitational possibility of developing new relations to it. It invites us to imagine how we represent disability as an external, medical condition that merely happens to a few people. In short, this version of disability studies invites us to imagine that we collectively imagine (create) disability to be *what* it is, to notice it, respond to it, and to interpret it in the way we understand it to appear. Such noticing, responding, and interpreting are also activities historically located in the politics of ruling relations – or, as Dorothy Smith suggests (1999a: 98), theorizing needs to address 're-ferring, representing, inquiry, and discovery as the locally organized social practices of actual people.'

But accepting such an invitation in the face of disability is not an easy thing to do. Understanding disability as a space of interpretive encounter represents disability differently and forms an imaginative relation that does little to further any bureaucratic project. It is much easier to live with disability bureaucratically, to understand it as an external condition with negative effects for some people or, as in chapter 2, a 'worst case scenario' for which special plans need to be forged. A more ambiguous and interrelated image of disability, in contrast, produces only a best case scenario – a society full of disability, a collective where people participate in reflexively imagining our differing orientations to the creation of embodied life.

The Problem and the Promise of Excess

Conceiving of disability as something gone wrong in an individual, detached from the movements of interpretive socio-political life, makes it easy to resist a disability studies approach.

> Look – a wheelchair user is a wheelchair user is a wheelchair user. And, well, blindness, what would I have to do with that? No imagination needed. Disability is rather obvious, isn't it? When I see someone using a wheelchair, it has nothing to do with my cultural location as a perceiver of disability images. The facts are that she's blind; and he is paraplegic; and I am not imagining this. Perhaps all these fancy words about culture and bureaucracy have something to do with those more questionable or invisible disabilities. Well, many of those people just need to get their acts together and stop using disability as an excuse. Everybody needs to get on with their lives and realize that either a person is disabled or not. Disability isn't a matter of perception.

Nonetheless, disability is ambiguous, as it is created by a collective imagination influenced by socio-political conditions and history. Thus, disability studies does have a rejoinder:

> But what did you perceive when you chose to notice the wheelchair? Titanium frame and lightweight wheels? Mobility? Confinement? Effort? Strength? Speed? Calamity . . .? How did you know you saw blindness? Do you see it always? Does it see you? When disability appears, did it appear to you in particular? Is it the same, are you the same, are you or I or we the same in the face of the appearance? Did you notice difference, devalued difference, devastating difference . . . and how about desired difference? Disability appears through the interpretive life of people living in cultures prepared for its own perception and not that of others. We have no access to disability that excludes cultural conceptions.

Disability is certainty, yet it is the certainty of ambiguity made incarnate. This is the promise of its excess; disability is not containable within the confines of its individualized appearance since that appearance is itself culturally organized and ordered. (Ironically, any ambiguous moment in Western[ized] culture can come wrapped in disability imagery, e.g., what's going on with this crippled economy and its lame jobs – it's crazy.)

Ambiguity and certainty – these are key images through which disability is represented and to which the politics of person-first language is a response. Person-first language seeks certainty, locating it strictly in personhood, in order to deal with the ambiguous power of disability as a life-shaping force – a force paradoxically regarded as empty of life. A sense of humanity abstractly and arbitrarily dividing certainty from ambiguity makes disability as dangerous as is the illusion of a normal human being, and such images seem to naturalize this artificial division between certainty and ambiguity. Representing disability as a condition added on to personhood, but abstracted from its life, does not allow disability to be enlivened nor give access to it as a necessary and meaningful part of human existence. As much as we desire to gain access to disability as a complex space of questions, it seems impossible to escape the notion that disability is, in fact, over there, objectively rendered in some other Other. Current warfare is replete with images of faces blown off, missing legs, and broken backs. Yet people who embody such injuries are rarely spoken of in person-first language and are instead rendered technically and statistically. This is as true for those spoken of as 'collateral damage' as it is for military personnel. These depictions of disability make it seem far removed from humanity by rendering it, with certainty, as other. The common signifier of disability – the stick figure in a wheelchair – does not enter the picture of disability in warfare or disasters. The certainty of the stick figure certainly represents disability; but those injured by war shake this certainty with ambiguity. What is certain about disability is that it is ambiguous.

But even if we do think of disability as war's number one product – according to the UN, there are three disabilities to every death – this abstraction requires us to locate disability in people, and in social and political contexts such as war. What remains? Every image of disability is an image of culture. By making use of the wartime ratio of disability to death, the UN urges us to imagine that it is normal to connect disability and death; as Lennard Davis (2006b: xv) has shown, disability serves as a *memento mori*. Moreover, thinking of disability in terms of a ratio requires us to invoke the concept of population where population means a variety of types of people – in this case, disabled people and dead people – each type expressed in rates. This logic both relies upon and reproduces a clear distinction between self and other that, in turn, relies on and reproduces a clear distinction between certainty and ambiguity – you are either dead or alive, disabled or not, this is the 'normal' state of affairs. The dichotomy between disability and non-disability is also perception itself, insofar as it is one of the things we co-create when we perceive. Disability is the activity of perceiving and thus representing how we orient to, for example, certainty and ambiguity. As we perceive through disability, then, all of us are intimately a part of what disability becomes in our perception. Disability exists in the midst of this perception, in the midst of people, and in the perception that flows between them. To understand disability as created in the liminal space between self and other allows us to address the confines of contemporary representations of disability, including the oppressive ones. This means that we can embrace the ambiguity of the inadequacy found in any representation of disability where it is depicted as objectively given – and, in perceiving such ambiguity, allow ourselves to wonder, and thus to begin again where all disability begins – in imagination.

Between Images

Through reflecting on what disability is and its various representations, we have developed the alternative position that disability is made in the socially organized space of imagination that exists between people. Within this space, images of disability circulate in culture. This is why disability is always steeped in the cultural act of interpretation. Cultural representations of disability are typically expressed in definitional form – in legal terms, policy terms, medical terms, and in other everyday terms. Examining, rather than tacitly relying upon, these definitions reveals disability as an imagined form of embodiment, usually devalued, but always living in and inhabited by culture. It is in culture, in the midst of others, that disability is made; in this way, we are never alone in our bodies (Titchkosky, 2007a). This remains true despite the consumeristic orientation of medicine and education that conceives of the human body as property: *Alone* in my body as my property and sometimes my problem, I had better do something about my problem body. Whenever and however disability appears, and since it appears in culture, we can examine the normatively grounded cultural meanings from which our images of disability arise. And this leads to new questions.

How do we and how might we relate to these images of disability? In the face of disability's ambiguity we often resort to categorization.

We categorize it as, for example, good or bad, positive or negative, or as oppressive or liberating. Across North America safety campaigns by worker's compensation, by Mothers Against Drunk Driving, and by the War Amps Children's Fund all use disability and death in order to frighten people into working safe, driving safe, playing safe (Michalko and Titchkosky, 2010). Such safety campaigns configure disability as the *horrifying exotic*, a haunting spectre, a way to show what can happen to those individuals who risk safety, who put 'normal embodiment' at risk. In contrast, other media images configure disability as part of ordinary life. Disability is figured as 'I can do just like you!' or 'We are all able.' This image of disability is geared towards convincing us that the noticeably 'abnormal' body can take part in the precious activity of doing things normally. Disability images can, paradoxically, bring together the neo-liberal values of 'Be safe!' and 'Just Do It!'

These images of disability are transported though the 'genre of normalcy,' 'a genre that specifically uses abnormal – impaired – characters to deal with a perceived threat to the dominant social hegemony of normality' (Darke, 1998: 184). In the face of many different ways of imagining and representing disability as certainty, one singular abiding outcome is the generation of a sense of normalcy as all-important. Disability representations, suggests Paul Darke (1998), are shaped by and supportive of a genre of normalcy. This genre uses disability to suggest,

> Be safe . . . in normal ways since it is normal to be safe! Just do it . . . but do it normally since it is normal to do things normally, just like everyone else! Actively do normal things in a safe and ordinary way. Take interest in disability, attend to it, help it, or otherwise represent it insofar as it serves as a reminder of the unquestioned good of normalcy.

Images of disability are also messages that can be creatively reread to expose the sort of work disability is imagined to do in contemporary times. The appearance of disability is expected to serve as a scene where people can imagine that normal is good, even precious, without ever having to think about what is good and precious about being normal. While 'normal' is a socially achieved status that does not imagine disability differently, understanding disability as an image that is made between people can occasion a desire to develop alternative images of normalcy and of disability. In his essay, 'What's Cool about Blindness,' for example, Rod Michalko (2010) provides an alternative image through his characterization of the everyday ubiquitous demand to set the time of disability to 'culture standard time.' Other alternatives can be witnessed in the development of cultural endeavours, such as disability sports and arts, where disability is imagined as something *other than* the devalued-other whose only good is an ability to support the reproduction of normalcy and its abiding power in the orders of daily life.

Theorizing, too, produces alternative images of disability.

Image and Theory

I turn now to theorize one of the most prevalent and taken-for-granted images of disability that we encounter in daily public life.

Typically, a white stick figure against a blue background, a symbol of a wheelchair user, serves today as the universal sign of access. While it is not titillating, this is a common and taken-for-granted image of disability and access found throughout North America. Still, even in this clear image of disability, the spirit of ambiguity resides: the existence of a universal sign for *access* is reliant on an exclusive and exclusionary physical and social environment. In order for a sign to point towards access, there must be an assumption of a general lack of access. Every universal access sign suggests that access is available only in particular locations. If access were widely available, signs of access would not be necessary. Insofar as this image of disability gains its sense by being situated *between* the promise of access and some knowledge of its absence, this ambiguous image *is* a complicated, even paradoxical, social scene. Of course, there are many other scenes where the normalcy of exclusion is figured through the image of potential access for people. Still, this stylized image of access is a good place to start to address the space between access and exclusion that is filled with the certain ambiguity that is disability. Here, the answer to '*what* is disability?' is, a paradoxical social scene where interpretations of disability are made

Figure 3.1: Wheelchair stick figure used to indicate access in Western(ized) environments.

manifest. It is paradoxical since the sign says access is certain, but only under the ambiguous social condition that it is not. In this sense, signs for access found sprinkled throughout Western public life are a pressing social scene in need of theorizing if we are to disrupt the ongoing perpetuation of the normalcy of limited access – and the ongoing social exclusion of bodily differences.

Access signs function only in the face of inaccessibility; inaccessibility can only be perceived when access starts to become a question; and access can become a question when it is present so as to structure perception. That some signs can point towards access requires the background expectation that access is not a normative assumption, even as the apparent promise of access is laced with need and with desire. Moreover, such signs are read by particular people variously oriented to the access/ no access to disability situation. Access signs give people a sense of the questionable status of accessibility. In the face of these signs, people access a sense of the normalcy of limited access as well as the need to seek out signs of its potentiality. Still, the signs must signify something of the everyday understanding of space and bodies which has led to their placement here and there – but never everywhere. What interpretive acts do we invoke when we notice this particular image of disability?

As a way to continue to address signs of access and environments of inaccessibility, I turn now to a narrative. The characters, events, and location of this story are a composite of actual characters, events, and locations which I use in order to orient to normal conceptions of disability as a place of wonder. As Native storyteller Thomas King (2003: 2) tells us, 'The truth about stories is that that's all we are.' So, I present a story as part of who we are.

A Story of Signs

I have started a new job at the University of Toronto. I start to teach new classes, meet new students, staff and faculty. I also start to help develop this university's disability studies program. I think it ironic that, given all that is new, what keeps me awake at night are those familiar little blue-and-white signs of universal access. I say to Buddy – that's the name of the man who is in charge of all the money for the institution where I work and who also maintains the building that I work in – I say to him, 'Hey, there is nothing accessible about that washroom, or about the back door to the building . . . it weighs a hundred pounds. Okay, I'm exaggerating. But to get through those doors you've got to be strong, agile, and you've got to be skinny, too. Buddy, I think that the signs really have to come down.'

He looks at me funny as if this is the first he's heard of it. 'But Buddy, you were at the meeting, faculty council passed the motion; it says inappropriately placed access signs are to come down. There are access signs on very inaccessible doors around here.'

Again, we go off to take a look at the signs while Buddy says, 'Look, isn't something better than nothing?'

I resent that this doesn't seem to worry him much.

Outside the back door to the third-largest building on this university campus, Buddy and I face this narrow, thick, and heavy wooden door with its access sign displayed high and in the centre. 'See,' I say, 'You're driving around. You spot the sign. It's like a message saying, "Here, come here, you can get in here!" So, you park. You go through the trouble of getting out your wheelchair or your walker, or whatever, and move toward the sign.' Now pointing at the blue and white sign, I say, 'You move toward here to get into the building. The sign is a beacon. It is like an icon of access. But there really isn't access here; the door is too heavy and too narrow.'

Buddy says, 'Why don't we just leave the sign up and put another sign up below it that tells them to go around the block to the front of the building?'

Anger rises. I think, how could he think this? I ask, 'Why hang on to a useless – no, not useless – *misleading* sign?'

'For many years,' Buddy explains, 'this was the only way into the building for anyone who had any problems.'

'Problems . . .' Yes, people have problems, but doors do not, and in this way the sign on the door appears as not a problem. Still, why not take down the sign now? Can it be that the icon of access can be pressed into service so as to honour a memory of an even more inaccessible time? Are these signs like grave markers of times when there were even more radical exclusions? What is the problem here?

Twelve months later – that's how long it took – the blue-and-white access signs are down in this building, but my trouble with them hasn't ended. I am starting to notice them all over campus. They are everywhere and they are bothering me. Big signs placed here and there around the entire square-city-block, angular edifice of the massive library. Now, Buddy has nothing to do with the money or the maintenance of the library. Still, the signs echo his recommended solution: each big access sign tells those who get close enough to go around the block to one particular entrance.[5] Then there are those blue-and-white access signs marking smooth, automated entrances into other university buildings, where once inside a person must go up or down stairs to get to any classroom; or at the top of a flight of stairs there is a door, and the door has an automated opener which nonetheless displays the icon of access. It doesn't seem legitimate to me that the universal access sign should be put to use merely to indicate an automated door opener. The Beer Store doesn't put an access sign on its automated door. These access signs make me imagine that lack of access, partial access, and partial participation are all being taken as normal, sort of expected. These signs announce that certain people are 'special' cases and indicate that limited access is sort of normal. How to make sense of such particularly modest, even miniscule, gestures marked by a *universal icon* of access, big, bold, and blue?

I count myself among the politically astute, but I am discovering a more poignant irony here than my so-called political astuteness first allowed me to grasp. These signs are not Buddy's fault; they are not even his idea; I bet you he didn't even put them there in the first place; and he certainly didn't put them in every other campus building. *Never till now* had it ever occurred to me that an organization would systematically display icons of access to merely indicate that there is a *possibility* that people *might* enter here, 'but no promises beyond that!' It did not occur to me that the universal icon of access would give me access to disability defined as partial participant, since barely 'in' is in enough. I know that my culture, including my new university, radically marginalizes people, including disabled people. And here is the grandest irony of all: I *completely* trusted this culture, this culture of exclusion, to come up with a really good, honest, and straightforward way to signify access.

But there's hope. It is becoming clear to me that I've been re-educated. My practical literacy skills have been honed and I can now read all the many blue and white icons of access for their functional significance. On this campus these access signs read: 'Here you can enter . . . *maybe*. But beyond your entrance regard yourself as a questionable participant: you may or may not get to classrooms, you may or may not pee, you may or may not visit your professors or colleagues. This sign means you are our collective's *partially imagined may-be*.' This is an ambiguous welcome – put up an access sign and a may-be-participant is made.

My relations to these images of access are sort of shattered – in fact, I sometimes feel out of sorts. The sign now marks a kind of distress. And what should be done with signs that are pointing to the ambiguity of belonging, the partiality of participation, the uncertainty of certain sorts of people?

Imagining Viable Difference

That is the end of my story. The truth about my story, recalling Thomas King, is that that is all we are. We are those who can use images of disability to repeat the past and to tell new stories, and that is who we are. We can also tell a story about disability access that can shake up a secure and certain sense that signs are doing what they say they are doing. This can be a little disorienting and it can lead to wonder. After all, we typically read signs as indicators, as giving information, as directing us to the required and the expected. Signs, in other words, are a form of orientation.

Sara Ahmed (2006: 8) says that orientations are 'about how we begin; how we proceed from "here" which affects how what is "there" appears.' The 'here' is clearly not accessible to us if we notice signs of access 'there.' Signs gesture and promise a way to go through a network of taken-for-granted background expectations. Like all other images of disability, signs recommend ways to live in the movement that is social space. It is, then, disorienting to find signs that do not fulfil their promise of direction. It is also disorienting to experience access signs doing the opposite of what they promise; and it is disorienting, finally, to experience access signs as bringing the background order of inaccessibility to awareness. We can imagine that every image of disability – good, bad, or merely practical – can end up pointing to the unexamined background order of normalcy as well as the socio-political order that sustains it.

'The point,' says Ahmed (2006: 158), 'is not whether we experience disorientation (for we will, and we do), but how such experiences can impact on the orientation of bodies and spaces, which is after all about how things are "directed" and how they are shaped by the lines they follow.' What kinds of bodies and what kind of spatial access are we directed towards by the ways we imagine disability? What kind of lines are we drawing and following as we tell stories to each other in the particular places where we concretely find ourselves? If disorientations are key to the vitality of opening up new ways of perceiving the meaning of access – and people and places – then we need to examine this taken-for-granted form of orientation. In the face of my dyslexia, for example, signs are always, potentially, a little disorienting. I know that they give direction by orienting bodies and space, but I don't know if I have read them in the way others have and this is disorienting. My disorientation presupposes signs to have a singular meaning of direction – it should mean only one thing. But that meaning is not clear to me – thus disorientation.

But recall that signs do not only direct, they also shape. They shape what we are oriented to and how we are oriented in the spaces where we find ourselves. Even if I get the direction wrong, I have nonetheless been directed to the expectation of the singularity of the sign's meaning. If we are 'shaped by the lines we follow,' then the dynamically different ways we might orient to access signs will have an impact on the interrelations between bodies that we have been, bodies that we are, and those that we will and will not become. Representations of the body, including icons of access, direct us to ambiguous or disorienting questions regarding the space of the body – and conceiving of people as partial participants has an abiding history of reproduction in the Western world.

My story of shattered expectations in regard to disability access images is more than me merely becoming conscious of false advertising. My story is about the disorientation of being directed to regard people (but not signs) as contingent, as partial participants, as living 'maybes.' Shaping bodies in space is a function of not only useful signs, but misleading and useless ones as well. Signs, including signs of access, appear as both meaningful and as meaning makers. The icon of access appears, and in so doing it appears as a sign of access made through the social expectation of inaccessibility. The meaning of the common practice of putting a universal icon of access on an electric door opener that opens only to a flight of stairs needs something more than to be identified and lamented – or laughed at. These cultural contradictions cannot be dissolved by simply saying its 'some-Buddy's' fault, nor is it resolved by saying that it is the fault of some bodies. In the face of the universal icon of access, it is instead possible to read a particular, even peculiar, call; the sign is calling out, 'Here is both an image of access and its opposite! Everybody is affected and shaped by this, so now what?'

Beginning Again – In Imagination

More is at stake than taking down signs, or people's motivations for not doing so, or moving signs to better places. As a representation of contradiction, access signs serve as a kind of cultural puncture since they make manifest the desire for the undesired; an inaccessible accessibility, a partial universality, and other paradoxical relations to space and belonging. Representing the intersection of access and inaccessibility, what this image is about is the orientation towards disability itself as cultural contradiction. Icons of access perform (Butler, 1997, 1993) disability as it has been made to mean under contemporary socio-political conditions. Such images mirror the normative order of the culture of which they are a part, from which they spring, and which they reproduce. Disability is other than an inability and more than a society's failure to respond to the presence of impairment; and it is certainly something else besides celebrated or degraded identity categories. What is at stake in the face of the question, 'What are we doing when we represent disability in this way or that?' is the need to theorize human embodiment. Asking what disability is when its representations make an appearance in daily life is a way to make the matter of normalcy itself disorienting and try to imagine that our lives as bodied beings could be otherwise. It could be different. Not only is disability structured as the partially imagined 'maybe,' the collective orientation that does this structuring can also be made contingent – made into a maybe. Maybe it, maybe we, maybe both image and the perceivers of those images could be different.

'Moments of disorientation are vital' (Ahmed, 2006: 157). This is a difficult idea to grasp, let alone accept, since disorientation is typically encountered as a distressing problem that we need to set straight as soon as possible. But 'vital' does not preclude distress. Disorientations are vital in the sense that they testify to the possibility of something new arising in the face of the same. The experience of disorientation points to the possibility of asking, 'How best to orient to our disorientation?' Given that the universal access sign often signifies the normalcy of inaccessibility, it is difficult to imagine how images of disability will ever stop signifying the normalcy of regarding some people as contingent. In an exclusionary physical and attitudinal environment, every sign in public space can be read as directing some people to seek access elsewhere insofar as they are made to embody a 'maybe' status. In fact, every image of disability can be considered for how it represents all sorts of people, places, and times as 'maybes.'

As a moment of disruptive provocation, there may be vital lessons to learn from this disorienting sign of access that is a common way of imagining disability. Perhaps Buddy, the man with the money who controls signage, is right . . . something is better than nothing, but only when that something is read as a demand to desire more. 'More' means trying to experience disability as a collision between imagination and desire, reflecting the meaning of our bodies in everyday life – and where that life puts us into relations with lines of history that came before us and that remain for further reflection.

I turn in the next chapter to this difficult task of imagining more by tracing out some of the ways that disability is normalized as absent within the university scene. I move to other narratives of the icon of access as it organizes relations between bodies and social space. Sometimes the icon of access confronts all bodies as 'out of place,' and, in the next chapter, I reveal what this has to teach us about how we interpret our bodies in the university environment. The questions of 'who?' and 'what?' are now leading to the question of 'where?' This is where I engage the human-made environment as comprised of a power to reference the making of versions of human. The question now is: what do we learn from *where* we do and do not find ourselves in the face of disability?

4 'Where?': To Pee or Not to Pee

So far, I have explored disability as a space for enacting a restless re-flexive return to consider the social meanings of embodiment.[1] Such an approach adds to the growing body of disability studies literature, a process of knowledge production different from the established knowl-edge regimes of cure, care, or containment for taken-for-granted notions of the body-as-deficit. Disability studies does not aim to improve the current knowledge regime's management of disability, nor does it seek to add yet more knowledge to this regime. Neither is it about enhancing the power of those disciplines firmly in control of disability knowledge production today. This is why disability studies does not treat disability as an individual biological matter, but rather as a social phenomenon requiring critical inquiry (Finkelstein, 1998: 33). Understood as a social and political entity, we come in touch with disability as an interactive space representative of the cultural environment in which and through which our lives as embodied beings always appear.

Sharon Snyder and David Mitchell (2006a: 198) tell us that '[h]istori-cally, disabled people have been the objects of study but not purveyors of the knowledge base of disability.' Methodologically, this does mean that being disabled makes one a vessel of knowledge. In actuality, knowl-edge, like disability itself, is socially organized. Disabled people are socially organized under the rubric of 'knowledge bases,' which are or-ganized by cultural understandings of what counts as knowable. There are many ways of knowing what disability is and who is disabled, as the previous chapters have shown. Insofar as knowing is steeped in its social location, then, the places from which we perceive and find disability are important to examine. This chapter aims to reorient *where* we can know disability by examining the places from which disability is perceived.

Within the everyday practices and procedures of university environments, for example, knowing disability as a 'problem in need of a solution' (Titchkosky and Michalko, 2011; Michalko, 2002; Oliver, 1996) is
knotted together with making disability appear as nothing more than
myriad undesired difficulties. To reorient what counts as knowable,
there is also a need to attend to the scene where the meaning of disability can be observed. When disability is no longer understood as located
in individual bodies (who?) or in administrative problems (what?), the
question becomes where to locate or base disability knowledge. It seems
obvious that there is an intimate relationship between establishing disability studies as an important form of critical knowledge production
within the university, and creating accessible learning environments
where learning communities can thrive. The development of disability
studies, then, must coincide with the development of a more inclusive
educational environment. As Snyder and Mitchell (2006a: 196) suggest,
'Disability studies must recognize that its critique should be trained on
the institution of the academy as much as on the social and political
context outside its walls.'

As the previous chapters have demonstrated, taking an interest in
improving access is reliant on questioning inaccessibility. This means
that access and inaccessibility are dialectically related and attending
to this relation is the place where many new questions arise. Between
access and inaccessibility lies a place where it is possible to theorize the
cultural configurations of embodied existence and come to experience
our interrelatedness differently. Insofar as access – and the fight for it –
is a space of questions, and thus a base for knowledge production,
many questions can arise in the midst of the interactional scenes of access struggles in educational environments. Not theorizing the obvious, yet intimate, relation between the environment and its participants
leads to an unimaginative relation to justice and scholarship. Theorizing disability's appearance as, for example, a justified absence makes
it possible to resist turning access struggles into a boundary-building
process where who is in and who is out is tacitly re-established.

In the following section, I examine the ordinary ways that body/
environment relations are articulated in the university. Ordinary talk
which justifies the exclusive shape of daily life is a way to explore how
meanings of disability are generated since such talk relies on unexamined conceptions of disability. I treat the use of taken-for-granted
conceptions of disability as one place where disabled people are made
absent, and where this absence is regarded as irrelevant. The *use* of unexamined conceptions of disability as a social power that reproduces the

status quo, even as the material environment changes, *is* a new space for the generation of knowledge. Working at the crossroads of the material and ideological production of disability, I aim to reveal access not as a synonym for justice but as a place where critical questioning can occur. I turn now to a discussion of the setting from which access narratives – that is, everyday talk regarding access – arise.

Where Access and Inaccessibility Meet

Again, my workplace is the setting for my analysis; first, let me say a few words about this 'where.' I work in a twelve-storey university building of 350,000 square feet. It is the third-largest building on Canada's largest and arguably most diverse university campus. The building's main entrance is ramped and the building has state-of-the-art elevators with audio indication (although the announcement of the floor number and the opening of the door are not well synchronized). I began to work in this building in July 2006 and discovered that there were no washrooms in my place of work that met either university or provincial minimal disability accessibility standards.

Ironically, some of these inaccessible washrooms were marked with the universal icon of access. One such icon, for example, was on a women's washroom door that opens about sixty-one centimetres, or twenty-four inches. This narrow opening meant that almost anyone trying to enter this washroom would have to nimbly squeeze through the doorway. I was disturbed by the lack of access. In the round of daily life, I talked to many people in this setting about the lack of an accessible washroom and the obviously incorrect signage. I did not set out to make this trouble into a research project and I was not covertly collecting data. I was, however, attempting to live with, understand, and ultimately fix a problem. Simply telling those in authority that the signs were incorrect did not bring the signs down. So, I tried to learn about how and when the access signs were posted as a way to get them taken down – and I attempted to figure out how this might relate to the absence of accessible washrooms and the possibility of changing that, too. As a newly hired disability studies professor these washroom quandaries became an essential aspect of *where* I was working.

Through the act of drawing attention to these barriers, I was given a plethora of stories regarding why there were no accessible washrooms, as well as stories regarding why such inappropriate access signs were posted. I was struck by the various *stories-at-the-ready* that are part of this workplace environment. Even as accessibility features of one top-floor

1958; Clough, 2002; King, 2003; McGuire and Michalko, 2011). The apparent and obvious ease of a statement like 'things just weren't built with people with disabilities in mind' is a way to make inaccessibility sensible under contemporary conditions. This ordinary 'truth claim' is a type of say-able thing in relation to disability that I have heard many times, in both rural and urban environments across Canada, and in reference to all sorts of structures. It is a comment so ordinary that survey data collection processes might never solicit it since surveys require respondents to reify ordinary experience.

Noticing and collecting things – especially ordinary things – said in the stream of daily life regarding the justifiable character of exclusion requires a different relation to 'data' than is usual in the social sciences. Narratives such as 'You know, I mean, things just weren't built with people with disabilities in mind' are so routine and common that it would be difficult to attribute them to a particular individual speaker. The mundane efficacy of the merely say-able allows such sayings to slip past individuality. Indeed, speakers of the say-able are perhaps better regarded as a conduit of types of cultural understandings. An understanding that the say-able is where cultural understandings reside is what grounds my methodological decision to return to and address the say-able, shaped as an amalgam of narratives. My data here is an amalgam, or a composite, of people's justifications for why in 2006 there was not a washroom in this large university building that met minimum accessibility requirements.[3]

I have created five stories, five say-able justifications, from a variety of comments encountered through my everyday experiences where I work. All the say-able things I recount in this chapter were said in the presence of others, some of whom sometimes treated these things as wrong or distasteful, but who were not oriented to see them as baffling. In this creative amalgam, sheer *sensibility* is what interests me. Thus, I have grouped or amalgamated fragments of narratives spoken by people to compose stories that represent typical ways of saying that exclusion is justified.

Insofar as everyday language can, following Alfred Schutz (1970: 96–7), be understood as a 'treasure house of ready-made pre-constituted types,' the 'whole history of the linguistic group is mirrored in its way of saying things' and there is no need to individualize these words. From an interpretive sociological perspective, all say-able things are representative of the cultural grounds of possibility from which they emanate; or, as Maurice Merleau-Ponty (1958: 214) says, every 'word is a gesture, and its meaning, a world.' Now that I have provided a justification for my use of taken-for-granted justifications that readily circulate through the rounds of daily life, the question is: What are our say-able things doing in the places where access and exclusion meet?

Here are five stories.

Five Stories

1 Some faculty and staff say that they fought hard, some twenty years ago, just to get a ramp for the front door of the building. They suggest that is probably when the signs of universal access were posted everywhere, including on inaccessible washroom doors. Once posted, 'How were we to know any better?'

2 People say that in the distant past, human rights lawyers used to rent space to meet here. It is said that some of these lawyers were wheelchair users. This group began to push for accessible washrooms. They failed and took their meetings elsewhere. Still, the inaccessible washrooms got the universal sign of access posted on them. A lawyer wonders, 'Maybe a cubicle inside the inaccessible washroom got a wider door?'

3 Those responsible for the building say that others keep talking about how students in wheelchairs are going to come to school here, but they never show up. 'Why go through the expense?' As for the signs being posted, 'Isn't something better than nothing?' Agitated by the suggestion that people are getting stuck attempting to enter these washrooms, someone pointedly reasons, 'If they can't use the washrooms *what are they doing* here anyway?'

4 Administrators, officially responsible for making structural decisions and allocating funds, say that they are working on it. You can't do everything in a day. In fact, maybe we need to just slow down. Thirty years ago, in good faith, the signs were put up and it is possible that, within a decade, we might be moving to a new building. 'Remember,' they say, 'we did secure the special fund to build a fully equipped accessible showcase classroom. Maybe some of that fund could be used to build a washroom?'

5 All sorts of people are perplexed to find out about the inaccessibility and that those in authority do not seem to take it as a crisis that we are working in a building that does not have a washroom

that the *particular* meaning achieved by these justification narratives remains a poignant question worthy of consideration if we are to re-think where we find ourselves. What, then, has been made sensible?

Including Disability as a Justifiably-Excludable-Type

The giving of reasons achieves the inaccessible washroom situation as sensible through a tacit reliance on 'including disability as an excludable type' (Titchkosky, 2003b: 518). The building is missing accessible washrooms and yet it is not; the building is not missing disabled people and yet it is. The building's missing washroom is made sensible through the seemingly justifiable conception of disability as excludable. Disability is included as justifiably absent, and when it is present it appears in the form of an unimagined or unwanted question, that is, 'What are they doing here anyway?' In such a situation, 'accessibility' becomes a space for reasoning how the appearance of missing disabled people can be accounted for as a reasonable exclusion.

The inclusion of disability as a justifiably-excludable-type is one way disability *is* represented in everyday life. This poignant paradox is not unique to my workplace. The phrase 'oh, she's gone on disability' attests to the structured ubiquity of the inclusion of disability as an excludable type. I am not arguing against disability insurance. Rather, I am arguing for a consideration of ordinary talk as a constitutive power making up the meaning of people. The power of this form of inaccessibility is demonstrated by the absence of disabled people in my place of work.[4]

Some ways of making disability present as reasonably excluded require an understanding of people living with disability as a justified absence. The conception of disability as a justified absence *acts as a barrier* to inclusion for some disabled people – a barrier that is not necessarily recognized as such. Unless the relation between environment and its participants is theorized and thereby disturbed, disability will continue to be included as an excludable type even as the physical environment changes. The discursive act of making something 'justifiably absent' ultimately has much to do with how we delimit the shape of possible worlds – or, in Judith Butler's (2009: 2) terms, justifying absence performs, and makes present, what counts as 'viable and non-viable' lives. This means that any conception of 'where,' such as the social and physical environment, needs to be understood in relation to things possible to say about it.

Acting like a little nail in the gap between the multiple stories of justifiable exclusion entails a restless reflexive engagement with these ordinary ways of living with the paradox of disability as an excludable type. I return to the justification narratives with the aim of finding some difference in the same (Bhabha, 1994); to live otherwise than ordinary (van Manen, 1990); and to offer an alternative relation to the alterity (Cixous and Derrida, 2001) in the discursive space that disability represents. The question now is: 'How does included-as-excludable appear as a sensible and justifiable understanding of the lives of disabled people?'

Extra-Ordinary Exclusion

The narratives display different ways to do justification while constituting a sense of place as well as governing relations between place and people. Through utilitarian cost-benefit rationality, through bureaucratic sequencing of tasks, through partial fights and unmade decisions – through these ways and many more like them, justification is accomplished. While the end results might be common to these narratives, the justificatory processes depicted in them are not. The third narrative, the one that suggests that disabled people are neither desirable participants nor imbued with rights, seems different; it is the most obviously egregious of the stories and sticks out as most in need of interrogation. Yet I am uneasy with focusing on where it seems most obvious to do so. I now proceed with this disquieting 'preliminary, inarticulate understanding,' as Hannah Arendt (1994: 310) calls it, of an obvious offense, as well as a need to seek the non-obvious in the obvious.

Again, the third story:

> Those responsible for the building say that professors keep talking about how students in wheelchairs are going to come to school here, but they never show up. 'Why go through the expense?' As for the signs being posted, 'Isn't something better than nothing?' Agitated by the suggestion that people are getting stuck attempting to enter these washrooms, someone pointedly reasons, 'If they can't use the washrooms *what are they doing* here anyway?'

In this story resides 'a treasure house of ready-made types' (Schutz, 1970: 96–7) – there are those who belong; those who do not; and those who can explain the situation of belonging to and for all. Professors are characterized as unrealistic, but are still oriented to as a type who belongs in the workplace. On the condition that they are not wheelchair users, or that they can use inaccessible washrooms, professors, like students, are part of this story since they are 'obviously' part of the university setting – they are depicted as belonging where they are. Professors who hold the expectation that disabled people belong in the setting, in contrast, are dealt with by raising the idea of false expectations. Wheelchair users are depicted as 'never showing up,' as an 'expense.' When they do show up, they are also depicted as a questionable type, that is, 'what are they doing here anyway?' 'They' are a type who does not belong and so can never really be present, but if present, 'they' are only questionably so, a 'maybe participant,' since 'something is better than nothing,' because nothing is the only alternative on offer. As partial participants, disabled students are typified as visitors who have overstayed their welcome, rather than as desired or necessary members.

Interestingly, story number three does not claim that it is unrealistic to have an interest in accessible washrooms in public buildings. The inaccessible washrooms are not the targets of this justification. Instead, the targets are disabled students; it is disabled students whose absence is justified and whose presence is made questionable. Notice also that disabled professors or staff members remain unimagined types. 'Students with disabilities' are taken as the type who do not belong and as never really present anyway. The type that does not belong, the disabled type, is far removed from the imagined possibility of belonging to any of the other 'ready-made types' common to this workplace, such as professor or staff member (Michalko, 1999: 41ff). All this combines to give a sense of where 'we' are, as well as how we are to be there – whatever else 'place' is, it needs to be understood as a governing power.

The third story suggests that professors have an unrealistic interest in disability since it is rare, transitory, not present, expensive, and only found in students of whom it is not clear 'what they are doing here anyway.' This story participates in rearticulating an extraordinarily common belief that disability is not only rare but is also nothing other than limit and lack, unexpected and undesirable, or simply 'trouble' (Abberley, 1998; Hughes, 2007: 673). This narrative, then, represents an extreme example of including disability as an excludable type where exclusion is *made* normal because disability is *made* not-normal. Disability is not normal, not imagined, not needed, not common, not necessary, and not going to come to mind as the type for whom buildings are built or services provided. Disability is not, as the saying goes, 'where it's at.'

Arguing against the inclusion of a type by invoking the type itself is a straightforward act of discrimination. The open discrimination of story three makes it stick out, but is there not some connection between this obvious discrimination and the other stories' more ordinary use of histories of the environment to narrate justifiable exclusion? What possibilities arise if we treat story three not as aberrant prejudice (a bad apple), but instead as the heart of the consciousness of embodiment in this setting?[5] Recall, as well, that the third story is composed of narrative fragments spoken among people who did not respond as if they were confused. If people are always a 'consciousness among consciousness' (Merleau-Ponty, 1958: xiv), then this suggests the necessity of treating what is said in relation to other say-able things, and not treating what is said as a symptom of a bad apple or some other individualized state of affairs. By resisting individualization of the say-able, the interrogation of the wider cultural grounds of embodiment can continue. Let us continue, then, to explore the contradictory sensibility of these say-able things about disability as this constitutes a sense of 'where.'

Dis-Education

It is, of course, empirically incorrect to say that people who use wheelchairs never show up, since they do. Even the obviously discriminatory third narrative acknowledges that people who use wheelchairs do show up. Still, all the narratives presented here reflect an environment where justification of exclusion is achieved by saying that disabled people are somehow not present. There are other seemingly non-discriminatory, say-able things that also exemplify the understanding that disabled people are not present: 'Well, I am sure those in charge of the building would stop saying such awful things if they had to deal with people in wheelchairs.' Once again, and not for the first time, it is important to recognize the conflation between the radical diversity of embodiment and the single iconic figure of the wheelchair user. The deployment of this icon makes disability into an 'easy read' by reducing the lived complexity of embodiment into a caricature – literally, disability-diversity becomes a stick figure. For my purposes, however, it remains the case that disability imagined as the wheelchair user is still a place where the meaning of disability can be theorized. Absenting diversity from the collective imagination of disability is one form of absence. But there are others. How else does making disability present as an absence make sense?

Saying disability is not here ends up working with absence as a useful presence. Saying disabled people are not present, even though they are, serves to justify a sense of a mythical absence while being part of the productive sensibility that maintains what is, the status quo. The myth of the failure of disabled people to show up sustains what Colin Barnes (1998: 65) says should by now be an unsustainable belief – that 'disability is a medical problem affecting a small proportion of the population.'[6] The logical contradiction between 'they never show up' and 'what are they doing here, anyway?' gains its sensibility through some yet-to-be-revealed conception of disability. This conception is undoubtedly connected to limiting disability to the image of someone who uses a wheelchair. This limited representation of who disabled people are is grounded in a conception of *where* disability is believed to belong. It must be this conception that disallows a collective from experiencing the remarkable situation of including disability as justifiably absent, while making the actual presence of disability unperceivable – or only perceivable as a question or stick figure caricature.

A variety of scholars have addressed the issue of the relation between conception and perception, or reception and possession, with regard to race (Ahmed, 2006; Bhabha, 1994; Dyer, 1993; Gilroy, 2000; King, 2003; Parekh, 2006). Paul Gilroy, for example, speaks of the connection between the perception of race and the production of racist structures. He says: 'The human sensorium has had to be educated' (Gilroy, 2000: 252). As David Howes (1991) says, the meaning of the sensorium is the culturally specific ways our senses are hierarchically ordered – with vision, for example, being dominant in the West. The notion of the sensorium is similar to the phenomenological insistence that 'there is no such thing as a simple act of perception since anything we are perceiving appears against a dense backdrop of past, present and future experiences' (Weiss, 2003: 27; see also Classen, 1993; Titchkosky, 2003a, 2007a). In whatever way we sense disability and make it sensible, it reflects the cultural education of the sensorium; it reflects the dense weave of historical experience that organizes perception and the relations among the senses, as well as conceptions of what the senses are good for. What a person senses does not occur in a linear fashion, as if through the body we go out to meet the world. Instead, through a dialectical tie between sense and sensed, organized by where people and places interact, we receive an education regarding what is knowable and thus sense-able.

So the sensorium has had an education. Between never showing up and showing up as a questionable presence, wheelchair users are conceptualized as outside the ordinary sensibility of what it would mean to belong to the university environment. This is one cultural meaning of disability that operates in this workplace environment. If the meaning of the presence of disability as a living absence was not already operating in the environment, the say-able things recounted here would not strike me or you as sensible.

Even if disabled people show up, they need not be perceived as doing so since the collective sensorium has had an education – or, playing on Gilroy's words, a dis-education. This dis-education teaches that the concept of legitimate participant does not include wheelchair users, and makes other forms of embodiment simply beyond imagination. The dis-education of the sensorium includes a way to sense and make sensible the legitimate participants with their legitimated 'normal' accommodation expenses: lighting, chairs, technology, privacy, directional signs, pleasing eye-scapes, and, of course, a place to pee. Legitimate participants rarely, if ever, confront access as a question since they can take for granted the 'normal' education of the sensorium to expect a massive infrastructure of and for able-ist consumption and use. The plethora of academic disciplines which study disabled people as deficit alongside the dearth of examinations of environmental deficit are also part of the dis-education of the sensorium. Thus, the hundreds of missing disabled students, faculty, and staff are not experienced as missing. The expected workplace participant is the result of being educated to not notice the absence of disability. Where we are, then, has much to do with what representations of disability can exist. Between these representations of both places and people resides meaning making where the sensorium, again, has had – and continues to have – an education. Finding ourselves in the middle of an education of our sensorium, the theoretical imperative to wonder about who, what, where, and when becomes crucial.

The dis-education of the sensorium, however, leaves some people unable to imagine that disability is, indeed, missing. That is, the sensibility of the five narratives relies on the non-presence of disability's absence. So, there is more to reveal about our collective dis-education through an analysis of ordinary, say-able acts of justification.

A Most Ordinary Story and Dis-Education

If, through the social act of giving justifications, the sensorium receives a dis-education, then we can reveal the significance of the story that strikes me – and, I imagine, other readers – as the most reasonable of the five stories: story number one.

> Some faculty and staff say that they fought hard, some twenty years ago, just to get a ramp for the front door of the building. They suggest that is probably when the signs of universal access were posted everywhere, including on inaccessible washroom doors. Once posted, 'How were we to know any better?'

This story suggests that access has been a battle that netted some changes such as a ramped front entrance. But other changes occurred too – namely, universal access signs were posted. The story suggests that it was difficult for people to know that they were living without an accessible washroom because there were signs that said otherwise. In a culture that makes vision dominant in the sensorium, icons indicating access in a visual manner are powerful organizers of how people orient to the environment. But what is working to keep people from 'knowing better,' or from questioning the social location of the icon's power? To suppose that disability 'just wasn't an issue and so just didn't come to mind' begs the question of what is making it sensible that disability is kept at bay and a disability consciousness is barred. As a way to address the questions that arise through a critical relation to the reasonableness of story number one, I turn back to the question of 'where,' which is where these stories arise. Let us reconsider the actual, physical location within which these stories are situated.

In 2006, this twelve-storey building had, among its more than two dozen washrooms, five washroom doors marked with the icon of access. Two of the five were on the main floor, and the icon appeared on both the men's and women's washroom doors. People who worked and were educated in this building witnessed wheelchair users getting stuck while attempting to enter the main-floor washrooms since there was a wall that immediately confronted whoever pushed open the door. Located among the many classrooms on the fifth floor were a men's and women's washroom, and the doors of both were marked with the universal icon of access. However, the woman's fifth-floor washroom 'accessible' door opened only about twenty-four inches, or sixty-one centimetres. In relation to the population that did (and currently does) have access to this building, many were (and are) likely to find that all the washrooms are a 'tight squeeze.'[7]

We can now get a fuller sense of the dis-education that the sensorium has received. The sensorium is so well dis-educated in this environment that the missing disabled people remain invisible, even as icons of access are continually displayed around the building and on posters and pamphlets advertising public events. But the dis-education of the sensorium is more powerful than this, since it reaches into the manner of bodily experience. Some people's own bodily activity of squeezing through the 'accessible' doorway is not perceived but this is not because this building contains a mob of aberrantly prejudicial people. Something has organized the possibility of not perceiving the contradiction between the access sign and the lived experience of using the doors. This dis-education has, moreover, left people feeling like they could not know any better.

The dis-education of the sensorium has included the sense of bodily touch in social space (proprioception), which now precludes knowing what a body can teach – namely, that these are very narrow doorways. The sensorium has been dis-educated even further since it is possible to not perceive how the body figures in space as a matter of belonging and participation. The dis-education of the sensorium, through the ordinary daily life of working in this building, has been a powerful one. The sensorium of a legitimate participant may not sense at least one of its own bodily activities in this social space; is unable to attend to the absence of disabled faculty, students, and staff; and is not set up to press for any more access, since its ability to perceive inaccessibility has been compromised.

'Where we find ourselves' is doing the work of enacting an alienation between self and social space. Questioning and theorizing the actual places where the sensorium receives an education reveals that the 'where' in 'where we find ourselves' provides a base for what can and cannot be known about the self. 'This is my space,' or 'I belong,' are sensibilities that arise not from a self that is secure in its own sense of self; instead, these sensations of place signify how space is made to anticipate some bodies by making some bodies anticipate their own fit. This anticipation of belonging comes along, in this case, with an inability to perceive what and who has been made not to belong. Thus, space governs. Where we are is a place that has already been made by a particular 'we' that is typically beyond question (Titchko-sky, 2010).

Because of the dis-education the sensorium has received, there is no readily apparent understanding of missing accessible washrooms as a crisis or as an emergency. There is, however, a suggestion in the fourth narrative that 'maybe we need to just slow down' and not waste time or money. In the face of disability configured as a justifiably excludable type – as an unexpected participant, as not really present or a mere cari-cature of the real – it is difficult to know what to do. Recall that even the lawyers in narrative two said that in the face of this *prima facie* case of discrimination they took their meetings elsewhere.

That which is say-able as sensible is a form of representation which has everything to do with where people find themselves and what they can and cannot perceive there. The power of justification to perform the acts of discrimination and exclusion is also an educative power al-lowing for a variety of ways of saying that disability is an unexpected non-participant or even a negligible entity. This suggests that the non-viable type is used to shore up the legitimacy of the viable type and this requires further examination.

Doing Ordinary Disability Relations

In 'On doing "being ordinary,"' Harvey Sacks (1984: 414) says:

> A kind of remarkable thing is how, in ordinary conversation, people in reporting on some event, report what we might see to be, not what hap-pened, but the ordinariness of what happened . . . Whatever you may think about what it is to be an ordinary person in the world, an initial shift is not to think of 'an ordinary person' as some person, but as somebody having as one's job, as one's constant preoccupation, doing 'being ordinary.'

Sacks suggests that the most remarkable thing to consider is that in the goings-on of daily life we have as our job, as our constant preoccupa-tion, ordinary ways of being ordinary in the face of what might best be characterized as extraordinary events. Why the third-largest building on the largest Canadian university campus lacked a single accessible washroom in 2006 will likely remain a remarkable mystery. Still, fol-lowing Sacks, it is even more remarkable to notice the various ways we have to report 'not what happened, but the ordinariness of what happened' and make the remarkable appear ordinary. Moreover, the ordinary stories that are at the ready and that people use to justify the current state of affairs are part of the job of building an ordinary life for an ordinary sense of self.

Through everyday conversations, we perform ordinary ways to orient to or relate to happenings, and the giving of justifications serves as one such way to report on what happened. Justifications of inaccessibility have done the job of transforming the startling, the extraordinary, or the wondrous into ordinary events, thus achieving a sense of ordinariness for both self and others. This means that in justifying extraordinary barriers to inclusion, we can do the *work* of achieving the appearance of being an ordinary person. What does being an ordinary person taking an ordinary interest in the workplace environment entail?

The work that the narratives of justification can be understood to be doing is that of making it ordinary to not regard the absence of an accessible washroom as a noticeable barrier. The washroom is not missing; *what is missing is any need to attend to such a barrier to participation.* Justification, with its inherent lack of alarm, helps to achieve the reasonableness of not noticing the missing accessible washroom and keep the obviously incorrect signage from coming to collective attention. No one is responsible only because there is nothing to respond to – the absence has been made absent and, moreover, ordinarily so.

Still, making absence not-noticeable requires work, ordinary work, and sometimes a lot of it. Lack of alarm or surprise, lack of a sense of emergency or even shame, helps to keep the non-noticeability of missing accessible washrooms, or of access signs on inaccessible doorways – as well as the non-noticeability of all the missing disabled students, faculty, staff, and administrators – from coming to attention. It is, after all, ordinary to not notice what is taken to be irrelevant; it is even more ordinary to not notice our own complicity in the constitution of irrelevancy. Social contexts represent a frame for the realm of the noticeable for us; it is the doing of being ordinary to stay within that frame, and show others that we are doing so, and thus doing the job of being ordinary.

It is, however, also part of the ordinary normative order of Enlightened times to say that one cares about disability. Indeed, disability is a category of interpretation that historically emerged as a way to collect all sorts of people as the 'deserving poor,' who through no fault of their own didn't 'fit' the ordinary workings and doings of industrial capitalist systems. Caring for disability is an ordinary doing which helps to gloss the contradiction between the appearance of the icon of access on washrooms and the lack of a need to attend to the actual exclusions and social meaning of the icon.

As contradictory as it may seem, 'disinterested caring,' or better yet, 'careless caring,' is an ordinary way for people to achieve an ordinary relation to disability. A gesture towards the act of caring, such as placing an icon of access on a door, poster, or pamphlet, is sufficient, since worrying about how we care about disability would not be an ordinary way to do the job of addressing what is otherwise barely relevant. It is sometimes said that due to lack of knowledge, or lack of comfort, some people end up speaking loudly to deaf or blind people; silently holding doors open for blind people; recommending barrier-riddled paths to wheelchair users; and other such forms of interaction. These kinds of interactions seem to ignore the particularity of an impairment while focusing on the fact that something should be done in the face of disability. Outside of a psychological rationality, there are other ways to make sense of this form of interaction. Noticing that which is typically regarded as not present, the ordinary job of engaging in the act of careless caring – an inattentive attention – manages to attend while reproducing disability as excludable. Awkward treatment of disability is a routine form of orientation in the flow of daily life. Instead of saying that disability disturbs and disrupts the routine order of daily life, I am suggesting that the routine order of daily life needs to orient and frame disability in such a way so that all stays the same. Disability does not necessarily disrupt. Rather, the ongoing job of doing being ordinary requires that disability be oriented to as disruption – and careless caring is one way to actualize disability as disruption. Returning to the washroom situation, noticing the excludable or the irrelevant is not ordinary, so that 'carelessly' using the universal icon of access does the work of dis-attending to disability while gesturing toward a caring inclusion (Titchkosky, 2009a, 2007b).

Not being alarmed in the face of radical exclusion is doing yet another interesting job on behalf of the ordinary, to which I will now turn.

Spending Time Being Ordinary

The doing of the ordinariness of not being alarmed is achieved by attending to time. One way to ordinarily respond to building structures is as signifiers of time, which is attested to by the disciplines of architecture, history, art, and so on. In many fights for access, 'historical oversight' is a rhetorical device suggesting that something is old, structured by old standards, and too expensive to change, and so nothing is done while maintaining the ordinary sense that the overseer would care to change things if it were not for this stifling history. But this rhetoric does not work so well in the situation that I am analyzing here. Unlike the 'building is too old' justification, the justifications in circulation in this particular building treat as given the building's relative access, as well as the importance of placing icons of access here and there. They also treat as given the sense that, 'well, you know, this building is far better than most other buildings on campus.' These say-able things do not ordinarily fit with saying that the building is an antiquated representative of the historically structured difficulty of inclusion of disabled people in the present or in the future.

A different sense of time nonetheless justifies this inaccessible state of affairs. This sense of time does not necessarily report on 'what actually happened' but it does help make normal the ordinariness of not really noticing that there are no accessible washrooms – or, if this is noticed, it is also ordinary to not be upset or worried. People's efforts over time have made changes and will, in good time, effect more change. This evolutionary version of time, almost void of the need to think of human agency (let alone human rights), is organizing a sense of the ordinariness of not worrying about inaccessibility. Mentioning twenty or thirty years into the past, or the need to slow down, or a decade into the future, does the job of indicating the 'not-necessary-to-notice' status of the inaccessible washroom situation. These ways of talking about washroom time seemingly transcend an ordinary sense of washroom use as an urgent and universal matter. 'When you've got to go, you've got to go!' has become 'When you've got to go, you've got to leave.' Speaking about a past or a future in the language of ten, twenty, or even thirty years does the job of showing that it is ordinary to not regard this as an emergency situation; this is a situation that has evolved slowly over time and can be expected to devolve in the same way. But what is the ordinary object that is given by this patient evolutionary framework?

Perhaps the object served by this patient evolutionary framework is 'modern Enlightened man' – it is the doing of the ordinariness of colonial, capitalist powers as these give rise to the formation of subjectivity. The modern colonizing subject, and likely the concept of 'person' under modern conditions, or what Bill Hughes (2007: 681) terms the 'normative invulnerable body of disablist modernity,' needs some sort of boundary. At the edges of this boundary resides the possibility of defining and shoring up belonging and not belonging, relevancy and irrelevancy, personhood and its Other. Disability, in this instance, can be characterized as the abject underside of legitimated existence, included as an excludable type by signifying it as an always-absent-presence. As a living paradox, the place where we do and do not find ourselves, where people do and do not represent the issue of disability, is intimately connected to a historical set of questions regarding the meaning of being human. Educational and environmental access issues are a space where the question of what it means to be an ordinary person who is oriented to as ordinarily belonging are implicitly worked out and sustained.

Re-Thinking the Stories We Already Are

Starting from the presupposition that there is no good reason for disabled people to be structured out of education is what made possible my critical engagement with who and what is 'in.' In this chapter, I engaged talk about physical accessibility in educational environments and examined the social organization of disability as an absent presence included as an excludable type. Instead of treating 'access' as a substantive state of affairs that an organization can possess, I imagined access as a space of say-able things where questions of embodiment can be pursued. That bodily experience is achieved through everyday talk about some other body's absence suggests the need for a critical, restless, and self-reflective way of living with the stories we all already are – and have already become. This self-reflective, interpretive turn gives rise to the need to examine the way we make sense of each other, to tell a different story about inaccessibility, and to learn a little more about the interpretive issues faced both by those excluded and by those who are presupposed to be legitimate, viable participants.

From my privileged position as an expected participant, my desire to not reproduce justifications of the absence of accessible washrooms animated my need to address lack of access beyond its rationalization. The more ordinary ways of narrating exclusion as justifiable serve as a poignant occasion for theoretic attention where representations of viable and non-viable participants can be exposed, interrogated, and perhaps come to be understood in new or different ways. The extraordinary act of exclusion, understood as an ordinary fact of daily life forged through contemporary societal endeavours, serves as a place where the stories that we are can be revealed and new narrations of ordinary lives can be told. Attending to how exclusion and marginalization are already narrated and how they manage life is where we might reflect on how we make the ways we do not live together sensible and ordinary. Thinking through narrative fragments that justify exclusion is, of course, another way of living together. Our ordinary ways of talking about what is justifiable play a significant role in making up the meaning of lives, and the doing of ordinary life supports the extraordinary activity of discrimination.

Every fight for access (or against it) is also an interpretive space in need of theorizing, since access is always tied to the production of daily life as embodied beings. Even when access is conceived of as secured, the question of interpretation remains. The struggle to secure access, like the act of barring it, relies on the historical interpretive milieu that made this struggle possible in the first place. Theorizing the struggle for access provides for the possibility of disrupting this milieu; building an accessible washroom also disrupts this milieu. This means that speech that justifies the exclusion of disability can be regarded as an opportunity to examine how disability is brought to consciousness under contemporary conditions. Perhaps we can begin to remake that which has conditioned consciousness by telling a new story about who and where we are.

The next chapter turns to some of the recent bureaucratic measures taken to include disability in university life. I want to engage these programs, measures, and projects so as to uncover the historical grounds of the ongoing history of excluding disability. This will serve as a way to address a fundamental question – namely, what sort of human history is being forged when we do and do not notice disability?

5 'When? Not Yet': The Absent Presence of Disability in Contemporary University Life

So far, this book has been oriented to doors, washrooms, and access signs – as well as conceptual and procedural structures of university life – as places to question the relation between embodiment and social space. Such structures are also spaces where the everyday act of educating and being educated are spoken about and accomplished. Structures are neither static nor accidental but are, instead, social activities; they carry messages about collective conceptions of people and places, conceptions which themselves come into existence through such social structures and activities. Life may have its accidental happenings, its oversights or mistakes. Still, that the meaning of the stuff of everyday life is forged, persists, or even changes means that structures can be regarded as living representations of social conceptions. Insofar as structures are taken as representational places, we can question *what* is made of the people *who* we encounter in the spaces *where* everyday life is accomplished. In this way, disability can be addressed as someone, something, or somewhere that is best understood and examined as existing between us as a question of historical location and cultural production. I move now with these 'who, what, and where?' questions towards a further question, 'when?' This is the question of history. Of course, it is the case that the question of historical location is behind all human activity, but here I engage it as another way to focus on access struggles.

'When?' – when do and when don't people or institutions proceed with noticing disability? What does it mean to find the time to notice that which was not noticed at another time? In the time of noticing, what might we come to learn not only about access, inclusion and exclusion, but also about the time/space relations that help to produce such noticing? A tacit assumption behind all these questions is that there is an important relation between the time taken to do something and the framing of time by the structures of daily life. Put in more phenomenological terms, 'existence is for us essentially linked to time' (Levinas, 1996: 12).

Through all the 'W' questions ('who, what, where?' and now 'when?'), an abiding concern is how, under bureaucratic governance including legislative or procedural change, disability remains more or less represented as an unexpected participant. How might we deal with the paradoxical fact that bureaucratic changes regarding access and disability policy can actually be a time of no change within some structures? For example, despite changes to both the bureaucratic policy and procedures organizing accessibility and accommodation issues at the University of Toronto, the rate of disability among faculty and staff has remained very low, around 3 per cent of the working population. This rate has remained more or less unchanged since the university began collecting employment equity statistics in 1996. At that time, faculty and staff who reported to have a disability represented a rate of 4.6 per cent of the working population at the university (University of Toronto, 2002). This high of 4.6 per cent is still remarkably low when compared to the general disability rate within the Canadian population, which ranges from 14 per cent to 17 per cent, depending on what organization conducts the count (Canada, 2004, 2002; Jones, 1994; Prince, 2009, 2004a). One way the 2002 University of Toronto Equity Report makes this discrepancy in disability rates sensible is by suggesting that more than 75 per cent of those reporting a disability were tenured full or associate professors who likely retired by 2002. An implication of this account is that despite bureaucratic tracking, management, and the development of procedures and offices to address faculty and staff 'with disabilities,' little change to the relation between place of work and conceptions of disability has occurred.

So, it is not as if there is simply the subject of disability meeting the objects of space, policy, attitudes, or barriers. It is, instead, that subject and object exist in modes of relatedness that endure; that take time, occur in time, relate us to our times, and represent the time of reflection. Exploring these assumptions through the movements of daily life makes 'when?' a question that can reveal the character of contemporary times as it organizes embodied existence in the places that we find ourselves. The turn towards the question of time is a turn towards a history of the ordinary moment of *now* – narratives of generation and perpetuation of the presence and absence of disability's inclusion and exclusion in contemporary university space.[1] Through the question of 'when?' there resides yet another way to engage with what I have been calling a restless return, to reflect on the relations between bodies and social space.

More fascinating still is that one of the results of the inclusive measures initiated by the university is the reproduction of more of the same exclusion. Yet it is difficult to find any university document that addresses the issue of its reproduction of 'what is,' namely, disability configured as a not-yet-fully-present type. This leads us to wonder – how do we come to regard disability as something that can be present as relatively not-yet-present? Interrogating everyday articulations of 'when?' leads towards understanding how the concept of inclusion can act to exclude, and how we might begin to resolve this paradox in new, more viable ways by beginning to wonder about how we make up the meaning of people within everyday Western contexts.

The Time of and for Bureaucratic Measures

The kind of time I am most concerned with is bureaucratic in character. This is the sort of time that is measured out in terms of the development of policies, plans, programs, and procedures that aim to address a problem in a consistent and unified fashion through regularized use of rules. This is what Max Weber (1947) refers to as the orientation of rationality (chapter 1). The time of bureaucracy might be plodding, but it is also usually assumed to be progressive, productive, and especially predictable. It is the time for 'making the same' – the same measures for those regarded as the same sorts of people who are similarly qualified for the same orders or offices of highly regularized participation (Stiker, 1999: 136; Diprose, 2005: 249). A bureaucratized notion of equity, for example, entails implementing measures so that those regarded as qualified participants are not excluded from university life on the basis of prejudicial beliefs regarding race, ethnicity, sexuality or sexual orientation, gender, religious or group affiliation, and many other categories of discrimination, including disability. Insofar as 'people with disabilities' can be noticed and understood as 'the same as' any other potential participant but still excluded unnecessarily, or excluded through no fault of our own, bureaucratic measures are developed to address this problem of excluding those deemed to be the same as any other includable type.

These measures appear to be oriented towards the goal of a higher level of inclusion in a predictable fashion.

Some yet-to-be revealed conception of disability organizes the time of noticing inclusions or exclusions as this relates to the university's more exclusive hold on defining qualified participants, or those who might be deserving of new rules of inclusion. Thus, inclusive bureaucratic measures are trickier questions than they may at first appear, since there are disconnections between what the measure intends to ensure and what is actually accomplished. It is possible, after all, for rates of participation for disabled people in the university to decline, despite equity 'policy to ensure' that the opposite is implemented. What kind of time is disability granted under the global reach of bureaucratic rule and what becomes of disability in these hyper-bureaucratized times?

These questions serve as testimony to the social fact that bureaucracy remains one widespread way of organizing attention to the issues of disability and access. After all, for those immersed in its workings, the inclusion and exclusion of disability is occupied and controlled by bureaucratic practice. This ordering also exceeds the confines of university space. As I showed in chapter 3, there is a global(izing) bureaucratized approach that treats disability as conditional and so people become persons *with* 'restrictions or inabilities to perform an activity considered normal for a human being due to a loss or abnormality of bodily structures or functions' (WHO, 1980). The global reach of bureaucracy is demonstrated by its consistently singular expression of disability that all but erases the radical cultural diversity of embodiment. Ruled by person-first linguistic expressions, all disabled people are regarded as the same sort of people who happen to come along with a condition of impairment; embodied differences along with race, gender, and sexuality are thus made to disappear. The process of bureaucratizing embodiment suggests that it is fair, or morally correct, legally efficacious, or even tacitly neutral to regard disability as a condition attached to some people while disregarding the ways disability is differentially conceptualized around the world. The programmatic structure of 'inclusion,' animated by the bureaucratization of life, is the space-time relationship within which it is possible to return to the question of the meaning of people as well as our essential interrelatedness (Foucault, 1978: 25).

The concept of inclusion is being widely used and treated as a self-evident good by contemporary Western(ized) universities. And yet, disabled people are so often, and in so many ways, excluded from significant participation. This fact also grounds the need to continue to address disability representation as something that can tell us about the present history of disability – that is, it can tell us about the 'here and now.' The questions of when disability is regarded as essential to include or exclude, how this work gets done, and when we come to actually live the question of 'when?' find import in that history – as Elizabeth Grosz (2003: 15–16) reminds us – is 'happening' and connected to what was and what will be. For now, let us continue with this history of the ordinary present by tracing out some of the recent moves being made on behalf of disability.

What's the Problem?

While disability makes many different appearances in university life, it also appears through a paradox, hinted at in the previous chapters and now more fully explored. The paradox is this: the presence of disability almost always fades into an absence, and in many ways a dominant depiction of disability is that it should appear as if it is not present, not appearing. Rod Michalko's (2002) analysis of the dominant taken-for-granted Western belief that the best difference disability could possibly make is no difference serves as a reminder of the ongoing, normative demand that disability 'ought not' make a difference. In the realm of politics and policy, ruled by bureaucratic order, Michael J. Prince (2009) shows the precarious status of disability shaped as an 'absent citizen.' I too am interested in how disability is made into something that does not yet figure as an essential participant by tracing out in a variety of bureaucratic endeavours the ways disability is included as a potentially excludable type in university life.

The interesting thing about legislation oriented by an inclusion mandate (and its implementation into policy and plans) is that all such practices not only need to be fought for and carried through but also lived – which means they are being interpretively addressed. So, the problem is not only the paradox of including so as to exclude; it is also a lack of wondering about how bureaucracy conceives of disability as a problem that it is endeavouring to include and yet is successfully making disappear. Let us now consider bureaucratic procedures and policies that are happening at the University of Toronto and at other universities in order to map what is occurring when acts of disability inclusion are launched.

Exhibit A: A Document Governing the Relations between Faculty and the University.

Article 9: No Discrimination

The parties agree that there shall be no discrimination, interference, restriction, or coercion exercised or practised toward any faculty member or librarian in respect to salaries, fringe benefits, pensions, rank, promotion, tenure, reappointment, dismissal, research or other leaves, or any other terms and conditions of employment by reason of age (except for retirement as provided for in this Agreement), race, creed, colour, national origin, citizenship, religious or political affiliation or belief, sex, sexual orientation, marital status and/or family relationship, place of residence, membership or activity in the Association, or any activity pursuant to the principles of academic freedom set out in Article 5. (University of Toronto, n.d., Memorandum of Agreement between The Governing Council of the University of Toronto and The University of Toronto Faculty Association)

Exhibit B: University of Toronto Governing Council Statement of Commitment Regarding Persons with Disabilities, November 1st, 2004.

It is the University's goal to create a community that is inclusive of all persons and treats all members of the community in an equitable manner. In creating such a community, the University aims to foster a climate of understanding and mutual respect for the dignity and worth of all persons.

In working toward this goal, the University will strive to provide support for, and facilitate the accommodation of individuals with disabilities so that all may share the same level of access to opportunities, participate in the full range of activities that the University offers, and achieve their full potential as members of the University community. The University will work to eliminate or minimize the adverse effects of barriers, including physical, environmental, attitudinal, communication and technological barriers that may prevent the full participation of individuals with disabilities in the University community. The University will provide the members of its community with opportunities for education and access to information regarding disability and the University's policies on disability. At the same time, the University will endeavour to protect the individuals' privacy, confidentiality and autonomy.

The University re-affirms that all individuals are expected to satisfy the essential requirements of their program of studies or employment, while

recognizing that students and employees with disabilities may require reasonable accommodations to enable them to do so. The University is, as
always, committed to preserving academic freedom and its high level of
academic standards.

The achievement of the University's goal depends on the participation of
each and every member of the University community, including students,
faculty, staff and alumni, as well as their respective representative organizations. Each of these parties has a role in creating an equitable and
inclusive environment, as well as in the accommodation process and the
identification, removal, and/or reduction of barriers. The consultative relationship among the members of the University community is based upon a
shared desire for an open, supportive learning and working environment,
and a shared respect for individual rights and dignity.

Exhibit C: Graduate Student Association, Accessibility Committee, Mandate, 2008, Ontario Institute for Studies in Education of the University of
Toronto.

The Graduate Student Association Accessibility Committee is a GSA
standing committee. It will be struck at the beginning of each academic
year and will be comprised of departmental reps, a GSA executive member, and interested graduate students. The committee meets approximately
4 times per year over eight months of the academic year and reports to the
GSA Council on a monthly basis.

This committee was struck to ensure that accessibility is an ongoing
priority within the OISE graduate student community and beyond. The
GSA Accessibility Committee defines 'access' broadly and works to represent the multiple interests of our diverse community. Our mission is
to initiate and facilitate conversation about accessibility with OISE students, staff, faculty, and administration and to help facilitate transformation toward a more accessible environment for all. We are committed to
ensuring that OISE graduate student life, academic structures, physical
environment, and classroom practice and pedagogy is inclusive of, and
accessible to all students. The committee will work to address issues
specific to disability access, while working collaboratively to promote all
issues of access.

These three exhibits serve as a history of the present. They do not, in
any way, represent the whole of a university's response to disability
but they do represent things possible to say and things possible to do

to disability and access issues at this particular time. These documents have entered into my experience of university life recently. They entered not as relics of the past but as moments in the present; bureaucratic say-ables that make disability manifest.

Such documents enter, organize, and reflect the collective meaning of disability in ways similar to the justification narratives in the last chapter. I have yet to be invited to attend a faculty or staff meeting where it was announced whether or not the meeting would be held in an accessible space; or whether material would be offered in an alternative format; or any requests for participants to implement more inclusive practices, such as large-print handouts. This absence remains despite the assurances displayed in the above exhibits. At the time of this writing, some notices of meetings have now begun to include a contact number if accommodations are required as well as the phrase 'I will do my best to accommodate your needs.' However, apart from jokes regarding size of print and aging eyes, or stiff backs and uncomfortable chairs, faculty or staff meetings that I attend do not gesture towards the idea of needing to include disability in the actual spaces where university life gets done. Ironically, this is the case even when the meeting directly addresses disability. This situation remarkably mirrors disability's status in the list of prohibitive grounds of discrimination in Exhibit A. Exclusion from the university's non-discrimination clause is also a lived reality in the workings of university bureaucratic daily life.

In regard to university events that are advertised to students or to the wider community, the assumption of the potential presence of disability, or of access issues, *is often indicated.* The blue and white wheelchair icon of access is often found on posters that advertise such events; numbers for access information and occasionally ASL provision are noted; and sometimes notes regarding access limits are included, such as those that say that there are no accessible washrooms at this venue. These are common practices reflective of current history.

Between these two very different procedures – that is, between there being no assumption of the presence of disability in general faculty and staff events and some assumption of the opposite in regard to student or community events – there lies an interesting message. Disability and access issues are being included under the assumption that it is present but will also be excluded; partially included, for example, for those who may be receiving an education but not for those who administer or deliver education. This difference reflects the bureaucratic way of managing a sense of disability as partial participant, as not yet fully present.

This message regarding the partial inclusion of disability reflects a particular interpretive milieu which plays an interesting role in framing new accessibility endeavours. Consider, for example, Exhibit C, a graduate student association (GSA) accessibility committee which was constitutionally mandated by the GSA in 2008. The mandate of this committee is to ensure 'that OISE graduate student life, academic structures, physical environment, and classroom practice and pedagogy is inclusive of, and accessible to all students. The committee will work to address issues specific to disability access.' No such committee has existed in the GSA's history and I can find no other document that would suggest that such a committee exists in other Graduate Student Unions on campus. The Accessibility committee is a new, bureaucratically established move towards inclusion through increased access procedures. However, this new mandate enters and reflects the community from which it has arisen, and not only because it comes from and focuses on student access issues and concerns. After all, the mandate makes explicit that its interest in access addresses 'OISE students, staff, faculty, and administration' in order to move 'toward a more accessible environment for all' – as a way to actualize this 'all,' I was invited to participate in writing this mandate (and did). Nonetheless, operating in a bureaucratic environment that holds fast to a tacit understanding of disability as a 'student issue' can have the effect of making the new inclusive measures actually function as a sign of more of the same. Disability is not really fully present, but it is temporarily present in those who might seek an education. As temporary or partial, each attempt to actualize the commitment of the mandate can bring about the sense that disability and access issues must be started 'as if for the first time' again and again. A similar sentiment is expressed in Sara Ahmed's work regarding the implementation of race equity policy in Australian universities. She says, 'You end up doing the document rather than doing the doing' (Ahmed, 2007). The above exhibits regarding disability policy end up planning to do rather than doing, so that planning for inclusion becomes the doing.

Disability has been explicitly included in the University's November 2004 'Statement of Commitment Regarding Persons with Disabilities' (Exhibit B). This statement moves towards understanding disability as an important category of concern by saying, 'It is the University's goal to create a community that is inclusive of all persons ... In creating such a community, the University aims to foster a climate of understanding and mutual respect for the dignity and worth of all persons.' Again, the simultaneous presence and absence of disability is re-achieved. The worth of all persons includes not needing to say or point to disability as part of the worth of persons in the first place. This creates a climate of understanding that worth does lie in personhood; that all people are participants in personhood, but that personhood is not necessarily nor essentially tied to disability since disability can be left off only to be attached later in the statement.

Separated from personhood, disability takes on a variety of appearances in the rest of the 'Statement of Commitment.' Thus, these different appearances of disability can be read as related to the question of the worth of persons. Placing personal worth and the condition of disability side by side, the taken-for-granted assumption of personal worth generates disability in a variety of fashions. First, disability may form the basis for discrimination and exclusion, a condition that needs to be addressed so that the worth of personhood can shine through. Second, and related to the discrimination or stigmatization faced by disabled people, disability is represented as an essentially private matter requiring the worth of the autonomous individual. In developing more inclusive measures, the neo-liberal values of 'privacy, confidentiality and autonomy' remain key and such values need to be (literally) re-inscribed when dealing with disability issues. Third, disability is represented in relation to how the worth of persons combines with the potential stigmatization of some persons as non-productive. After all, the concise 'Statement of Commitment' demonstrates its own need to confirm that work expectations for faculty, students, and staff remain the same. So, while the worth of disability is not located in personhood, it is framed as making a person's worth questionable in regard to the routine expectations surrounding productivity norms. Finally, disability is shown to be protected by this bureaucratic measure that attempts to secure the university's commitment to the inclusion of people with disabilities on campus. The document makes the version of disability it also aims to protect.

'[The] University will strive to provide support for, and facilitate the accommodation . . . so that all may share the same level of access to opportunities, participate . . . and achieve their full potential as members of the University community.' Disability will be admitted into the same level of opportunities, activities, and potentialities, but only if disability can be seen not to disrupt the taken-for-granted worth of persons. Still, this 'saming' of disability is yet to be realized. For example, according to the Federal Government of Canada, '[a]mong adults with disabilities, 7% have a university degree, compared to 17% among those without disabilities' (Canada, 2002: 33). The bureaucratic attempt to remake disability into a figure that seems the same as 'all persons' has indeed made disability into that which is, at best, radically under-represented on this campus – and, at worst, has made it disappear altogether.

All this should lead us to wonder about how bureaucracy spends time attending to disability. There is more than a lament or complaint at issue here: there is the social fact that the very ways the time of disability has been bureaucratically managed within the university system does not seem to be of much interest to that same system. The bureaucratic formulation of disability can make disability disappear. The ideal behind the policy makes disability so well included into the opportunities and operations of education that it can appear the same as non-disability, or so goes the hope. Or, as Stiker (1999: 128) puts it, we remove the difference of disability and make it disappear by drowning it in the 'single social whole.' This makes equal opportunity an equation which renders opportunity only for those regarded as the same. The opportunities and operations of education are always already normal and good whereas disability is always already other, and so we attend to disability only to make it disappear into this (unquestioned) good (Stiker, 1999). Bureaucratic ordering of education transforms disability into its other, to be addressed through plans, processes, and policies of inclusion whose fulfilment is signified in the act of same-ing.

A history of the present requires that we continue to ask 'when?' – *when* does access arise as a question and how does this allow us to question the governance of participation and belonging? The question of 'when?' can expand imagination so that we can question the meaning of bodies in social space – and question how we might find the time to tell a different story regarding the inclusion of disability as an access question for all.

The Living of Bureaucratic Time[2]

'Our time,' which is occupied by the both obvious and dominant bureaucratization of life, is a key time to consider the constitution of the meaning of people as well as our essential inter-relatedness. What does it mean that bodies, minds, senses, and emotions are being managed under bureaucratic time? This is not a question oriented to fulfilling a desire to develop a better bureaucratic approach, but rather to wonder about what concepts of disability 'do' for a bureaucratic order that is typically regarded as a taken-for-granted good. The act of bureaucratization need not only be lamented or praised but also thought about as it shows the workings of Western(izing) culture. I turn now to a more detailed analysis of a narrative account of my university work life – to the actual way bureaucratic time is lived – so as to explore the paradoxical character of the bureaucratization of 'life and limb.'

This story begins at my place of work. Actually, this story begins where all stories begin: in collective imaginative relations to what is deemed story-able about people, places, and things. I begin with one way of orienting to places of work – as places where things happen, since they are places organized by times of inclusion and exclusion. Recall that I work in a large research and teaching institute, OISE/UT. This twelve-storey building has included basic access features, such as a fairly accessible front entrance way, since the 1980s. By 2009, the building also included two accessible washrooms as well as a more accessible food and drink kiosk, elevators with audio indication, and a few electronic door openers for some offices sprinkled throughout the building.

OISE is located in a province which is beginning to implement the Access for Ontarians with Disabilities Act – the AODA – an act passed into law in 2005 and currently being translated into province-wide, enforceable accessibility standards for five areas of daily life. These areas include customer services, transportation, information and communications, the built environment, and employment (AODA, 2005). These accessibility standards operate on the assumption that by designing and implementing bureaucratic procedures, more people will be granted fairer access to the services and activities of life. While the built environment and consumer products might not change, or might be slow to change, the procedures whereby more equitable access to services is secured for people with disabilities is a primary and explicit goal. At issue in regard to customer service, as well as information and communications, is the need for organizations and businesses to develop written workplace procedures that establish clear protocols whereby services, information, and communication are more equitably available for people understood as disabled. For example, if an office – such as dentistry, criminology, or student loans and awards – is inaccessible to disabled people, an accommodation plan needs to be established as a written policy so as to work towards access for all. This written accommodation plan and its actual procedure need to be communicated so that the provision of the customer service happens for persons with disabilities. This new law also establishes that people with disabilities must be informed of the temporary closure of essential services. Access for 'people with disabilities' to the same goods and services as 'everyone else' is the explicitly articulated goal of the AODA. The AODA also states that how this access is actually accomplished will be decided on a more local level, within the workings of the organization, office, or business. Thus, the Province of Ontario includes work environments that are beginning to think about their legal obligations to meet the AODA mandates. This climate is part of the context of my workplace.

But one more contextual aspect to my story; not only do I work in a university in a province that is beginning to implement an accessibility act, I also work with graduate students, faculty, and staff, some of whom use, would like, or otherwise need an accessible washroom. In 2006, there were no accessible washrooms in the twelve-storey building; in 2009 there were two such washrooms (main floor library and fifth floor). In the summer of 2009, administration announced plans to build an accessible washroom on the main floor to be open at all times, and this was completed in 2010.

With this basic physical and ideological workplace context in mind, I offer the following access story.

Once again, faculty ask, 'Will the community of OISE be notified the next time one of the accessible washrooms is closed down?'

The answer from administration is a very robust and very complicated 'it depends.' It depends, administration replies, on how long or how often it is shut. It depends on the washrooms that will be built in the future. It depends on whether people find it necessary to know; on who tells whom and when; it depends on who knows what to do; on who wants to know; it depends on where, why, and how. It depends on how the notification should occur – email, website, main entrance lobby notification board . . . it depends. Moreover, 'we certainly don't want to fatigue the community with any more email announcements . . . so, really, it depends.'

While community knowledge of washroom closures depends on a great variety of administrative or structural variables, it does not seem to depend on the fact that some people cannot attend classes, meetings, or other events unless there is a usable washroom. The emphasis on structural needs over and against people's access needs is noticed by some. So, faculty, staff, and students ratchet up the pressure. The communication of washroom closures becomes an issue before faculty governing council. 'How will the community be notified when the accessible washrooms are closed down?' It seems as if what is at issue now is a desire to wrest the answering of this question out of the control of those who say 'it depends.'

The aim becomes establishing a bureaucratic process that does not depend on what any one individual may decide notification depends upon. 'We want to be notified by email,' we argue, 'just like anyone else.' For example, just like this email:

> In order for the plumbers to complete urgent repairs, we need to shut off the hot water in all washrooms. We apologize for any inconvenience.

Or,

> Please ensure that all plants/nick-nacks [sic] are removed from the window sills . . . the contractor will not clean those windows where personal items are found.

Fire alarm testing; parking lot closures; heating problems, parades, or protests . . . all are announced, and the closure of accessible washrooms should be announced *just like* this, or so the argument goes.

But further complications arise. Various arguments are made against establishing a general procedure whereby the community will be informed about washroom closures. These arguments take some of the following shapes:

> What about email fatigue? Really, we get too many pop-up messages.
>
> Do all buildings have to notify if their washrooms are closed down?
>
> Do all washrooms receive such notification?
>
> There are two accessible washrooms now, it's not so essential if one is closed down.
>
> The AODA is going to be implementing across campus, in all buildings, we don't want to do anything here at OISE and then have to undo it. People might get their expectations up and what if we have to change once the AODA is implemented across campus?
>
> Are all buildings open 24 hours like this building? Do other campus buildings have to supply an accessible washroom throughout these 24 hours?

The AODA requires a lot of training for faculty and staff. We don't want to get in the way of that training; we don't have to comply until 2012.

But the arguments do not stop here since other questions reside within the issue of access. There is more to come from, for example, those who argue that it is essential that *all* people be notified if an accessible washroom is closed:

We are not just talking about access to washrooms here; we need to think about all matters of exclusion.

This is a wider issue, how else are we blocking students from participating at OISE, what about course outlines and assigned readings?

We should not just be talking about washroom closures! We need a more universal equity statement that includes disability but other equity-seeking groups too.

Hey, what about access issues faced by poor students, by racialized and trans students, by non-status students, flex and part-time students, by students with family obligations or language barriers?

So some argue for a more inclusive version of equal access for all; others continue to argue for a more inclusive version of the campus buildings, campus-wide policies, and universal procedures. The arguments on both sides, and everything in between, escalate. All this, despite the fact that the AODA (2005) customer service standard states, 'Provide notice when facilities or services that people with disabilities rely on to access or use your goods or services are temporarily disrupted.' Even though the provision of notice seems straightforward, it turns out that implementing such a standard in a bureaucracy is not so simple in the end.

These conflicts and tensions among all the competing arguments of what to do about washroom closures continue. And they do so despite the fact that all sides appear to be attempting to forge a good or reasonable bureaucratic response. What grounds this escalating complexity and conflict?

'It Depends': A Fascinating Relation to the Time of Disability

There is likely nothing unique in my story; this is, after all, the stuff of life that Hannah Arendt (1994) reminds us is daily food for thought. All who were engaged in this discussion of washroom notification expressed a desire for good bureaucratic management. All understood that access issues are the time of and for bureaucracy – which means that whatever is done will need to respond equally to all as much as possible. But it turns out that responding equally to 'all' involves what Paul Ricoeur (1974: 10) refers to as a crucial moment for interpretive inquiry – namely, a conflict of interpretation. This conflict of interpretation is not about whether or not washrooms are essential; nor is it about whether communities should be informed about essential services. The real rub of this interpretive conflict exists at the level of the notion of 'all.'

'Who or what is this community's "all" to which notification should be directed?' 'All' has much to do with the act of giving shape to 'notice.' How notice is given, about what, and to whom is part of an access argument where the meanings of persons are achieved. The ongoing argument on the part of disability rights advocates that the inclusion of the most 'severely' disabled is the most likely way to include the greatest number of people is not what is at issue here. What is at issue is the fact that the bureaucratic time for inclusion, the move to include all, is a productive space that organizes the perception of what shall come to count as a collective's version of 'all.' 'All' is as contingent a concept as any other way of referring to people. It is a regularly deployed concept when attempting to implement values and principles in a bureaucratic way – it is, for example, good for all people to know about washroom closures. Still, it is *essential* for some people to know of such closures. How do the 'some' for whom it is essential get framed in relation to the 'all' for whom it is good? How are the differences between 'some' and 'all' managed within the time-scape of bureaucratic procedures that are supposed to be oriented to the value of doing things in the same way for all? To live bureaucratic time is to live through an organized order that provides ways to perceive 'all' but does so without making people attend to how we come to understand this 'all.'

In this access fight, disability is made to symbolize a destabilizing conception of 'all.' *This* interpretive conflict regarding 'all' is tricky to understand so I will try to map it. There is the *all* of all washrooms, all buildings, all over campus (a structural all); there is also the *all* of all the rules and all those who make and enforce the rules (a procedural all); there is also *all* professors, all students, and all staff, who are all the people who are already receiving too many emails (the taken-for-granted, imagined collective of 'all of us'); there is as well the *all* of all disabled people whether they use accessible washrooms or not (not yet an all, but instead a particular type, those particular others for whom notification may be essential); finally, there are *all* the matters that relate to education and equal access for all (an ideal or universal all that seeks to go well beyond accessible washrooms and those who may need or want them).

Which 'all' are we or should we be talking about? Who or what organizes collective, imaginative relations to conceptions of the 'all'? The conflicting interpretations of 'all' ground the possibility of an argument over notification of closed essential services. Should notification procedures be consistent and applicable for all buildings all over campus? Should notification procedures be consistent and applicable to all people who enter the building, or just to those who pay fees, or just those who are official participants? Should notification procedures be consistent, applicable, and responsive to all matters of equal access, which includes access to services and offices, to information, class content, as well as movement to, in, and around the built environment? Or maybe we mean to speak of an ideal 'all' – if the issue is equal access for all, then washroom notification is not sufficiently general enough to warrant its own particular bureaucratic administration. It all depends. The expansion *and* the contraction of the conception of *all* plays a role in the bureaucratization of embodied life, and 'all this' means the official implementation of 'no change' – at least *not yet*. The 'all' of *all those who are actually blocked* from participation when there is a washroom closure without notification, is the all that is most quickly lost in the discussion of all the other matters.

There are many versions of 'all' on campus that do not yet include disability. So long as disability remains a 'not-yet' category it is possible to build an accessible washroom – and then, perhaps, the lock breaks and people say, 'We don't know what to do.' It is possible that for more than two months the one fully accessible washroom in a building could have a hastily scribbled sign attached to it, reading 'Out of Order,' with no alternative posted. This is a possible scenario not because of an evil group of workers; this is possible because disability (even as signified by an accessible washroom or as students ask about the washroom's status) is not yet essentially present. Thus people can say, 'Unlike with the regular washrooms, we didn't know what to do.' Knowing and not knowing what to do are not natural states of affairs; they are informed and socially organized by the dominant conceptions of the day. One dominant conception is that disability is a category of partial inclusion steeped in an ambiguous status as a not-yet. Disability is not yet something to which a community needs to respond, at least not all the time.

Even as the AODA is being implemented and access must be changed (by 2010, by 2012, by 2025) – even as conceptions of disability as a legal matter requiring response become part of all Ontario workplaces – disability remains imagined and configured as the not-yet. The actual embodied reality of students, faculty, and staff who provoke a consideration of the built environment and its communication almost disappears in the arguments regarding equal access for all. Perhaps embodied particularity is not a containable bureaucratic matter, but disability is incorporated as not-yet fully present – disturbing, since it is not yet taken as part of the all. It is not that somebody cannot attend classes because there is no accessible washroom; it is instead that disability, unlike window cleaning, is not yet imagined as an essential aspect of all of our lives. Disability is managed as a potentially excludable phenomenon since it is present as a not-yet.

How does disability regularly materialize (Butler, 1993: 32, 2009: 5) as a not-yet where the bureaucratic principal 'generally applicable to all' ends up actually including disability as an excludable type? All the structures, all procedures, all people already present, and even the ideal of 'all' itself somehow manage to include disability as an excludable type. A consequence of bureaucratic global occupation is not only that particular lives need to be made to fit into the bureaucratic type, but so does almost every form of practice (including who tells whom about what). A further paradox: the AODA has already fully spelled out what to do about closed washrooms and other essential services. The procedure of what to do in the future replicates, but does not address, the concept of disability that has already been delivered from its past, and so the competing meanings of all and the ongoing exclusion of disability remain untouched. Notification practices remain blocked since disability, configured as a not-yet, becomes a time where (at best) plans will be made to address plans to be made. Is this a bureaucratic SNAFU – that is, situation normal all fouled up? Or is this the normal and reasonable outcome of disability incorporated as a not-yet by excluding disability from all competing conceptions of 'all' – is this 'situation normal almost fully unified' (again, SNAFU)?

Still, this is not about treating disability as a naturalized problem in need of better bureaucratic management. This is about understanding disability as an interpretive category, that of the 'not-yet' kind, and this is difficult. Disability is with us and in us all at both the symbolic and material levels, and is so at all times . . . but disability is not yet recognized as a present and important participant. Disability is apprehended as a problem for bureaucratic organization and thus is in need of a bureaucratic solution; this requires the act of same-ing where 'person' can shine forth over and against any difference disability may make (Michalko, 2002). As a category of interpretation, disability comes with the possibility of becoming a not-yet; included so as to be excluded, present and yet absent, a not-fully-present-troubling-presence. This constant ambiguous status is a key feature of the kind of marginality that we come to face when we face disability. It is not only that bureaucracy cannot deal with ambiguity incarnate, it is also that taken-for-granted conceptions of 'all,' all of which do not yet include disability as a key aspect, need always to manage disability . . . out.[3] Disability is present, but remains a time where we have not yet begun to realize that we all already have conceptions of disability, which are as of yet unexamined.

But there is more. In the words of Judith Butler (2009: 9, 10), 'Something exceeds the frame that troubles our sense of reality; in other words, something occurs that does not conform to our established understanding of things . . . [Since] [w]hat is taken for granted in one instance becomes thematized critically or even incredulously in another.' Through troubling the routine ordering of disability, people are offered the possibility of rethinking the time and place of people, bodies, and social space in bureaucratized structures of daily life, exported around the globe today. Disability studies emerges in response to, and as a way to thematize, the normative order surrounding disability in the university system. Disability studies examines the actual time and place that disability is currently allotted by these same world-organizing structures. Such an examination requires that we take the time for a restless reflexive inquiry – which hopefully will be as troubling to bureaucratic rule as is disability itself. The implications of recognizing that disability exceeds its framing is to turn to some instances in the history of the present, where disabilities (and disability studies) are showing up and enduring in university life as more than – or other to – a not-yet.

Critical Relations and Positions: Disability Studies at the Table[4]

I turn now to another version of time: the time of joining critical theoretical projects in university life and what this might mean for the new places in which disability is showing up, exceeding its frame. By attending to some of the ways that bodies are made to appear and disappear, and by pausing to wonder about these embodied appearances, the necessity of continuing to develop a dialogue between disability studies and various other critical approaches can be confirmed and encouraged. Pursuing a conversation between critical theoretic approaches, such as those of queer, feminist, and critical race theory, can provoke us to theorize the time and the place of disability in university life in new ways. This is not to equate the different political trajectories of these fields of thought – it is instead to be in dialogue. Disability studies is emerging from, and as a response to, conversations regarding belonging, power, and order that others have already begun.

How people do and do not think about accessing questions of the body and social space is related to the issue of 'positionality,' which can mean the identification of features of an inquirer's position in the world as these relate to the act of inquiry and subsequent knowledge production. But how the term positionality is interpreted and lived has much to do with how people do and do not desire to explore the meaning of bodies in social space. For example, a positionality committed to expressing identity politics may need a strict sense of the clarity of types of bodies as well as clear forms of belongingness in order to do the work of addressing the relations between bodies, social space, and identity. However, any identity politics still needs to forge the clarity required to pursue a politics based on sure knowledge of its identity category. Other than such sure knowledge, there is also the more ambiguous need to figure out how we are always doing something other than taking a known stance and asserting ourselves. This leads to the question of alternatives – how else might we think about positionality in relation to a desire to turn to other fields of critical inquiry? I'll begin simply from my own experience of being positioned.

I take interest in disability from my relations to my white, walking, dyslexic, eldest-born, self-identified east-coaster, spiritually knotted, sociology teacher, here-as-such self. Here I stand – literally – since I am, as Eli Clare (2002: 82) says, a walkie. And yet I could come up with other positions, and likely something else that gets me going and for which I am willing to fall. But the fact that we are in relation to the identity categories we are perceived to represent, either by self or other, is important to emphasize. It is possible to get methodologically and theoretically animated not because we *are* an identity type but because we can and do think about, and live differently with, our relations to these types. This relation can position us – that is, the consideration of how we have different *relations to and with* all the things we *identify as* is a form of positionality that is essentially in process and open to wondering, even about its own position. We don't just stand or sit in our identities and choices; we inhabit them – and they inhabit us. When I read and write these sentences, taking them into little bits and reading the bits back against each other, while trying to discern if every part of a 'normal' sentence is actually in the sentence that I am attempting to write, I am inhabited by dyslexia while cloaked in the protective privileges of white professor. The difficulty of melding the sentence, making it mean something close to my intentions, and figuring out what I might intend in and through the act of writing means that I know that words are never certain. Normal/not normal; part/whole; intended/unintended; reading/writing . . . meaning is forged through a relation to these dichotomies, and that relation is another way to understand positionality. So, here and there we live, among different interpretations of self that are composed from multiple relations to the terms of our engagement, various political commitments, and diverse forms of inquiry. And, insofar as there is wonder, we can do and be otherwise.

This version of positionality – asking how do we position ourselves in the face of that which seems to already position us in schemes of identity and difference? – is a version of 'being positioned' that attempts to treat seriously the lessons that can be found in pursuing the question of 'when?' When do we take interest in disability; when do we seek to order disability under a bureaucratic paradigm; what happens to the meaning of disability within this time-scape? Such questioning supports, and is supported by, a turn to the historical processes grounding the actual making of the present moment; a focus on relations between perceptions of self and other. No one can *be* a type without being historically located, which means that types of people exist in a particular moment of time when they are recognized as such. The 'type' of person we are is not up to us alone since we cannot be alone in or with our 'type.' Thus the act of recognition by self and other combines to produce not only an appearance as a type, but also relations to that type.

With respect to this key form of interrelatedness, conversations between critical forms of inquiry and disability studies need not begin from an explicit act of self-identification nor from a strict act of identifying differences and similarities between theoretical orientations. I am following, then, a suggestion made by Ahmed (2006), which can also be found in the work of those critical traditions that take human interrelatedness as their beginning point – traditions such as phenomenology and hermeneutics. Ahmed tells us that conversations that we *can* have are related to the *tables* that we find between us. Positionality is not just about being types of selves, nor is it only about traditions of thought. Positionality is also about *tables: material paradoxes that come between people even as they bring people together.* The table can be read as a metaphoric rendering of Homi K. Bhabha's (1994) 'third space,' a kind of between-ness[5] that is important to think with and 'in.' In the third space it matters what people can find between what otherwise seems like clear divisions, or dichotomies, including those between 'self' and 'other.' Considering the tables that are between us is a little different than announcing identity since it requires one to disengage from a belief in an isolated 'I' that acts as if independent of others.

Considering what lies between us, Ahmed (2006: 43, 44) suggests, requires a focus on the table – on that which 'affects what we do' – a focus on where we tell stories from. It requires a consideration of the table space between us where 'how things come to matter . . . through and in the labor of others' makes an appearance. We are an effect of the tables between us. This is not a denial of self-identity but rather a radical social interpretation that locates the 'I,' the subject, in the actual time or movement of everyday existence. This social conception of self is never just 'mine' or 'hers,' despite any claim to the contrary.

On What Do Tables Depend?

Tables depend on labour and resources in unequal situations of production. There is the labour that makes the table, buys the table, places the table, arranges and cleans the table; there is also the labour involved in situating ourselves around some tables and not around others. The tables between us today are made by the labour of many people. Where I work, for example, doing disability studies includes the work of others who have secured a table (or at least a place at the table) called disability studies. This is a table that was forged by many and includes the labour of Professors Peter Sawchuck and George Dei. Before that, other students and professors laboured to establish disability as something other than a position of lack in need of remedy. Professors along the way here – including Kathleen Rockhill, Catherine Morgan, Sherene Razack, Kari Dehli, Catherine Church, and Geoffrey Reaume – all suggested that the meaning of disability is good to think about. All these people and others worked towards the establishment of disability as a legitimate area of inquiry within the institution.

Following Ahmed's suggestion to regard positionality in relation to the tables we find ourselves at, I am going to focus on Sawchuck and Dei's endeavours to harness the resources of the university and work towards the establishment of a table of disability studies. These professors applied to a special university Academic Initiative Fund (AIF) for a disability studies faculty position as well as for over half a million dollars to change the built environment of OISE – and build, among other things, a state-of-the-art and technology-endowed accessible classroom. The AIF is a one-time allocation in order to secure people, things, or events that are shown to be important but are absent within the university's current structures. The table of disability studies became much more solidly established through the AIF since material resources that endure over time, such as a redesigned classroom or an established faculty position, remain even as people actually positioned at the table can change dramatically from year to year. This disability studies table may be understood as a material paradox, a solid shift that brings together through putting something between us.

In the midst of the labour of many people, a sense of who people are comes to the table since people are also the *effect* of where we find ourselves. Such a self, interpreted as the effect of tables, means that my *here* today has something to do with my *there* tomorrow. I not only *come to* a table, I also *come from one*, and this is how tables affect what we do and who we are. Tables tell a story regarding where we can speak from, and even tell of whose labour we are willing to acknowledge as part of our social relations. Tables tell this story insofar as they are in every way related to representational places where we can question *what* is made of the people *who* we encounter in the spaces *where* everyday life is accomplished. Tables speak of our historical location even as they depend on this for their existence.

Regarding how we might be positioned in relation to this historical located-ness, there are many different tables made through the labour of others that have ordered the kind of universities we find ourselves existing in today. One particular kind of table is the type that is made through a direct relation to the *labour of response*; the labour of response includes the ongoing work of responding to other table makers, such as patriarchy, racism, and classism. The necessity of the labour of such response has, of course, not ended. To be invited to a table means to be recognized as belonging there in some way and thus privileged through the order of that normative expectation – and positioned as a representative of this normativity. Still, there are clearly some tables that have been built because something was not yet present, perhaps even absent, and this response to a university's version of a not-yet can make for interesting table talk regarding who is positioned to speak for what issues.

It is possible to merely announce one's positionality and it may be true that *what* I identify myself to be is generative of what I say. But, at the very same time, *where* I achieve those articulations of self has a great deal to do with what the act of identification will mean. Of this, Ahmed (2006: 50) says, 'The table is both the effect of work and what allows us to work.' How I say who I think I am is connected to where and when the work of identification happens. Where we do the work of identity is always situated between people in particular contexts, that is, at the tables between us, where history happens. Where I speak from is not only a position *of* a particular self, it is also a space from which such talk has been made historically possible.

Table Talk

Exploring the meaning of being at tables is to do as Hélène Cixous (1998: 87) suggests, namely, to address how we can experience an 'inner marginality' – the space, the rub, 'between my belly's skin and my trouser's waistband.' Between belly and trouser or table there is much that is good to think about, since this is where we think from. In order to address what is between the belly and the waistband, or the elbow and the table, I turn to a story. This is a story that clearly illustrates the material paradox of the table as it brings us together and keeps us apart with questions of when we are close and when we are distant from the meaning of disability. These questions happen at tables that have something to do with disability in university life.

In 2008, Peter Singer, a Princeton philosophy professor who is well known for his arguments for ending the lives of disabled infants, was invited by the *New York Times* newspaper to write Harriet McBryde Johnson's obituary. McBryde Johnson (1957–2008) was a disabled American lawyer and writer. She wrote 'The Disability Gulag' for the *New York Times,* and throughout her life was a passionate advocate for disability rights and was opposed to the killing of disabled infants. McBryde Johnson and Singer had occasions to debate each other on these life-and-death matters. For example, in 2001, Singer[6] argued that it would be good if parents could legally 'decide, in consultation with their doctors, to end the life of a baby when the child has disabilities so serious that the family believes this will be best for the child or for the family as a whole.' In the face of this 'best-to-be-dead' argument, the disability rights organization Not Dead Yet sponsored McBryde Johnson to debate Singer. Ironically, McBryde Johnson represented the sort of embodiment that Singer assumes that parents in consultation with doctors might consider as only worth letting die.

Singer and McBryde Johnson had other occasions to engage each other, too. In 2002, Singer invited McBryde Johnson to Princeton University. It was this visit – in particular, a meal at a restaurant table – that Singer ended up writing about when he published his obituary of McBryde Johnson:

> After she spoke, I arranged for her to have dinner with a group of un- dergraduates who met regularly to discuss ethical questions. I sat on her right, and she occasionally asked me to move things to where she could reach them. At one point her right elbow slipped out from under her, and as she was not able to move it back, she asked me to grasp her wrist and pull it forward. I did so, and she could then again reach her food with her fork. *I thought nothing of the incident,* but when she told some of her friends in the disability movement about it, they were appalled that she had called on me to help her. I'm pleased that she had no difficulty with it. It suggests that she saw me not simply as 'the enemy' but as a person with whom it was possible to have some forms of human interaction. (Singer, 2008: MM34, emphasis added)

Singer thought nothing of this incident; what he did think was that it was surprising for others to be thinking about Harriet McBryde Johnson's position at the table. McBryde Johnson did much thinking about being at this table with Singer, writing about it in her book *Too Late to Die Young,* and in her articles 'Unspeakable Conversations' and 'The Disability Gulag.' If, like Singer, we think nothing of the tables we find ourselves at, we might not come to know about the actual labour we are involved in – such as making the meaning of people or judging which lives are worth living and which not – and we may not recognize what sorts of conversations it is possible to have and those sorts of conversa- tions that are not yet realizable.

True, as the saying goes, 'stuff happens' – bellies rub, elbows slip, tables appear, invitations occur, and tables and people also disappear. 'Stuff happens' because of the particular tables we find ourselves at and because of how we orient to a table's labour. Not much happened for Peter Singer since he did not see the point of thinking much about being at the table. Singer says that he thought nothing of the incident except that he had set the table with his students, and at this table he reflected on how he had achieved his status as not just the enemy, but a person deserving of human interaction. Singer's status as a person was not in question since he is describing how he 'thought nothing of the incident.' Perhaps what was achieved was his sense of McBryde Johnson being human enough to see that he, Singer, was the human he was all along. And this becomes the *stuff* from which Singer creates McBryde Johnson's obituary. Still, being at tables, where bellies rub and elbows slip, where 'stuff happens,' is not justification enough for not thinking about the stuff that happens. After all, history is happening (Grosz, 2003: 25). The history of devaluing disability as a way to bolster the value of non-disability was dramatically reproduced by Singer not only at the dinner table but also at the table where the obituary of McBryde Johnson was written.

Turning to the University Table

Part of how the history of colonialism, patriarchy, and racism has continued to happen is through the idea that stuff merely and accidentally happens, especially at the level of the everyday. The material reality of tables now in university environments, such as those built by the labour of queer theory, aboriginal studies, and critical race theory, can be read as the history of response to what has for some time been regarded as a mere accident or even natural happenings. Within these critical theoretical endeavors resides table talk oriented to de-naturalizing marginality by exploring its historical production. Disability studies is also emerging in dialogue with this sort of table talk while problematizing the possibility of actually pulling up to, sitting down at, and partaking in the stuff of tables within the university environment. It is to the concrete material reality of actual tables in the university environment that I now turn.

Let us consider those tables we can actually experience in daily university life. In this realm of literal tables it is possible to continue to explore an inner marginality – the space, the rub, 'between my belly's skin and my trouser's waistband' (Cixous, 1998: 87). Between us in the here and now – for example, at OISE in the new 'disability' classroom space, in the library, in conference rooms – there are tables, new tables, tables where we are starting up some new conversations. There are now new tables at the University of Toronto and at universities across North America – tables on wheels.

It may seem all too ordinary to turn to the actual tables that we can find between us. Surely Ahmed, Bhabha, Butler, and Cixous, who have made people perceive race and gender, queerness, politics, and feminism differently, would not be pushing us to think about the tables we literally find between us. But the questions of access that a disability studies perspective offers make this move to theorizing the tables between us not only imaginable, but also desirable, since we are in the space where what is not yet fully present (disability) can begin to appear differently. And people in different positions at the table ask, 'who is at the table?' or 'when might we come to the table?' in a different way than those who have come before them.

Tables on wheels are seemingly opposite to the heavy, unmovable, regal tables that served as stolid signifiers of the North American university structure and its European past. Tables on wheels are now a part of collective university life and thus a part of collective imagination – and even expectation. We have seen or felt such tables, sat at them, worked at them, talked at them. Now we should also think about them.

These new tables on wheels were not at OISE a few short years ago; only recently could people enter the space of the classroom full of wheeled tables which can also be folded up and rolled away, all of this accompanied by a massive entourage of wheeled chairs. These wheeled tables and chairs make for desirable, even glorious, flexibility of classroom space, conduct, and practice. The desire to have university educational space *as* flexible space has meant that this 'wheely-ness' is becoming a common way to experience learning, at least some of the time and in some places. These tables speak of a collectivity's growing expectation for flexibility, where space is taken as adjustable to the bodily requirements of some of those bodies positioned as belonging in this educational environment. What becomes of both imagined and unimagined participants situated in classrooms with tables on wheels?

With these wheeled tables, representing the labour of flexibility, it seems at first that there is little tension, no rub, nor inner marginality between self, other, and the space of these tables that needs exploration. Perhaps there is just the pure, glorious experience of flexibility. These tables represent a growing awareness of universal design principles. According to designer Ron Mace (2008), 'Universal design is the design of products and environments to be usable by all people, to the greatest extent possible, without the need for adaptation or specialized design.' Wheeled tables support this principle of universal design and flexibility of space changes life chances for some bodies. These tables, like all organized space between us, affect conceptions of who belongs as well as the work we can do and the stories we come to tell, not to mention the stories that we can become. *Flexibility*, moreover, is a value intersected by the labour of anti-racism, feminism, aboriginal studies, queer studies, and disability studies since these traditions have worked to expand and twist the normative conceptions of who belongs, as well as the types of conversations that are possible – or even what counts as an area of research. At the same time, however, flexibility is a term that has a special value within the space of bureaucracy. Flexibility of process is often a stated bureaucratic desire as much as lack of flexibility is an explicit concern.

Given all these different ways of valuing flexibility we are clearly not dealing with a measurable, objectively given substance. Instead, 'flexibility' is a way to orient to some actions as valuable for achieving a desired end. This means that it is not so much that the tables are flexibility-incarnate as it is that they are being recognized as valuable, and in this recognition there is a yet another story to reveal regarding the relation between people and places at this time.

Tables make certain stories possible. If this is true, then so is the flip side: if tables make certain stories possible, they make others impossible. As both narrative possibility and as narrative limit (Cohen and Weiss, 2003: 1), tables affect the sort of work we can do. Even in the face of flexible tables, we remain as the effect of the tables found between us. As long as the wheel has been around, its meaning has stayed mysteriously complex. Consider the wheel's role in industry and transportation, for example. The wheel, as in the motorized vehicle, is tied to the leading global cause of impairment and death, especially among so-called developing countries. We need only think of the hard core capitalist commitment to car culture – our wheels – alongside the devastation of millions of peoples' economic, bodily, and earthly well-being, to recollect the very complex meaning of the wheel (Featherstone, Thrift, and Urry, 2005; Keohane and Kuhling, 2004). The value of flexibility gives rise to material realities whose stories reach and flow far beyond a mere reiteration of a desire. Like the wheel, our taken-for-granted values informing flexible educational university settings are more and other than 'what society made us [them] and believes us [them] to be' (Stiker, 1999: 51). So, let's turn the tables on flexibility. Let us consider what sort of bodywork is being done in the space that is inhabited by teaching and learning, situated among an ever-growing number of wheeled tables.

Recall that at this particular university, the Academic Initiative Fund (AIF) was a key part of establishing the disability studies table. It was the AIF which made for new classroom space filled with tables with wheels. These tables in the newly built 'accessible' classroom are formed from the historical understanding that space is needed to develop disability studies as well as include disabled people. Desiring to question 'normal ability' as a troublesome ground of belonging, I pursue here a disability-studies-informed ethnographic description of this wheel-endowed educational space.

The elevators open, and a second later the elevator's softly spoken voice says, 'Fifth floor. This elevator, going up.' It is 2008, we are off the elevator heading towards a classroom where the graduate disability studies course, 'Doing Disability in Theory and Everyday Life,' is being held. People are moving, in different ways, and with different mobility devices, down a long, wide, spacious corridor. Device-less, I am walking towards our new classroom. Some people seem to know that and follow me; I feel relieved that there is no way for me to turn the wrong way – I know the way. Moving towards the wide, spacious corridor, I am greeted by a wave of voices since the corridor is filled with students sitting on the floor. I assume these are people from ongoing classes who are now engaged in small group activities. The corridor is filled, as well, with tables on wheels, their table-tops folded down and pushed to the sides of the corridor. There are also a few chairs along my way as I weave towards the classroom situated at the end of this corridor. The corridor is now both an impromptu class-room and an obstacle course. I say to a group of students sitting in a circle, blocking the hallway from all who might not nimbly-foot-work their way through, 'There are students coming who use canes or wheelchairs.'

'Oh, we know, no problem, we'll move for them.'

'I mean, if they need us to, we'll be happy to move.'

When, I wonder? I continue to weave my way towards the classroom and see that the wide door is being propped open by a big, round table. Mobility devices or not, everyone entering the classroom will have to perform a wide, arching sweep to get into our 'flexible' classroom. I do so and stop. I look into the spacious classroom. Deep in this newly built accessible classroom space is a well-organized, neatly arranged rectangle of seminar tables. My look spotted the order that I expected to find here.

But between me and that ordered seminar space lies the rest of the room, strewn with tables all at different angles to each other. The well-ordered seminar seating is situated in a muddled sea of tables and chairs which are blocking the way. Until somebody moves the tables on wheels, some people can't get to the well-ordered inner rectangle of seminar seating. In fact, some people might not even be able to get in the classroom until this stuff is moved. I think, 'Luckily, there are enough of us who will be able to move tables, chairs, and garbage cans.' Then I realize that I have just begun a graduate level disability studies course not only affected by able-ism but also by my active deployment of it – 'some will move stuff for others who cannot.'

How is it that the very thing necessary for diverse participation is, in fact, blocking everything but for the most 'normal and expected' (least flexible) forms of participation? These moveable tables and their assumed tie to the production of flexible educational space have made for classrooms strewn with obstacles so that few people are provided with ease of access and movement. This is more than a lament, more than a complaint for which we might take responsibility; this is also an incredibly fascinating paradox. The flexible and accessible tables between us are also barriers to participation. These tables are being worked with in such a way that they may be the very thing that is leading instructors to have groups of students work in the hallways on the way to the 'officially' accessible classroom. This means that students who are proceeding down to what was billed as the 'accessible classroom' must nimbly tiptoe between the legs and bodies of those who are doing their educational conversations on the floor in the corridor. A new normativity, a hyper one, is required for unimpeded movement leading to the production of bodies who others can ply with the favour of moving out of the way, happily, if need be. But who or what needs it to be this way?

To get the full, fascinating paradox of this, let me put it this way: the inclusion of disability into an environment that has yet to critically reflect on the meaning of this inclusion has led to a form of non-disability-flexibility being implemented that continues to exclude, marginalize, and stigmatize disabled people. Inasmuch as collective space is not yet a collective concern, it can be the case that people who are part of a class are actually blocked by the classroom itself. The university regards disability as an individual matter, making accommodation a strictly individualized issue. This conception of disability makes the barrier of wheeled tables irrelevant since individual disabled people should negotiate these barriers within the new normative matter of flexible classroom space for an unexamined student-type. To be disabled and to move down the fifth floor hallway to the 'fully accessible disability studies classroom' is, more likely than not, to have space working against you. Thus tables affect 'us'; tables are the effect of work and affect the kind of work people can do.

What allows for the possibility of an environment that procures flexible tables but has yet to think of the space and meaning of the body? How does this inclusion (flexible tables) and exclusion (not thinking of the body) exceed the meaning of its own origin?

Working Tables

Some tables – the table of patriarchy, of racism, and also the table of ableism – are achieved through certain kinds of labour. This is the labour of a particular kind of exclusion, accomplished by positioning some people as though naturally excludable. It comes to appear as if it is on the basis of the excluded themselves (and not the labour of exclusion) that people are regarded as naturally not here, or that, as accidentally bared, 'stuff happens.' It is not, for example, that we have set a chair at the table that does not suit you. Instead, it is that you do not suit any of our tables and chairs. Exclusion, regarded as both self-evident and the natural fate of the excluded, can be achieved in a myriad of ways. The feminist concept 'chilly climate' has long demonstrated the complex force of such exclusion. One difference between a chilly climate and an inhospitable one resides between being chillingly put down and being 'the unimagined.' Both, however, can be dehumanizing and deadly.

In an inhospitable climate, disability is constituted as the unimagined incarnate; the unimagined made flesh. Remember the cultural contradictions that arise from the relation between an inhospitable environment and a disability identity where people moving towards class are greeted as if they are a problem to which individualized solutions can be applied – 'we'll move, if necessary, for them.' Today it is still not easy to begin to imagine this as an 'able-ist' consciousness since in an inhospitable environment 'normal ability' is yet to be regarded as a socially produced phenomenon. This history of the present includes the possibility of routine acts that suggest that there are no structures, spaces, and practices that actively support some bodies and not others. The message given is that the flesh of the unimagined is still readily included as 'naturally' excludable, as not-yet part of educational times, and certainly not an 'all' to which people need or want to respond to all of the time. Thus, we will move, if necessary . . . if they actually show up.

In the face of wheeled tables and chairs making for blocked entrances, or missing, broken, or mis-advertised washrooms, cluttered classrooms, garbage cans in doorways, and wide accessible hallways serving as barrier-riddled, floor-seating-only-classrooms, it is still routinely possible to say:

'What are you talking about, what barriers?'
   'Stuff happens, this is an accident, a mere oversight.'
   'Why don't they just say something?'
   'Look, don't take it so personally, no one has any intention of hurting people with disabilities, we just didn't know.'
   'You don't want to legislate the use of space, do you?'

Indifference towards the absent presence of disability, the surprise of not realizing its presence, as well as justifications of 'what is' that surround disability today are the kinds of work that come to the table and sustain the space where disability is reproduced as excludable. This means that including some people as always potentially an excludable-type *requires work*. It takes work, at the table, to not think about the sorts of bodies that are included and enabled in this social space, just as it requires work to not imagine the sorts of bodies that are not included. Orienting to disability as a 'not-yet' holds the place and meaning of disability in university life in historical limbo.

From the framework of bureaucratized work spaces, it is likely that people feel better off when the body – any body – disappears. Catching a cold, falling off your bike, menstruation, sleepless nights, hot flashes, desires, any of this body stuff needs to all but disappear for the work of bureaucratic structures to be achieved. When the body does make an appearance, for example, in pregnancy; in matters of illness, injury, and disability; in stress, anxiety, or anguish; or as a need to take care of others, we are instructed to officially 'take a leave.' To take one's leave is the primary bureaucratic mechanism for managing disability today. Clearly, the historical need by many critical theoretical traditions to proclaim that 'biology is not destiny!' is still necessary today. History is happening and it entails a variety of ways of making the body disappear – and then making any attention given to this social fact of disappearance seem a little absurd, overly sensitive. Nonetheless, elbows slip and bellies rub, and this can signify a need for bodies to come to matter differently in social space. The 'not-yet' time of disability studies is finding some time when it belongs and so is the experience of disability. Let's turn the tables again.

Repositioning the Not-Yet

Disability studies can now be found at a few more tables and is experiencing more chances, and even invitations, to participate. It is participating especially at those tables built through the labour of response – tables such as those built to critically address colonialism, patriarchy, and the normalizing processes of medicine and neo-liberal governance accomplished through bureaucratic procedures. These are the sorts of tables disability studies is making an appearance at, in part, because it is the effect of what others have laboured to build. Yet, being at these tables still includes an inner marginality and disability studies is not necessarily at one with those at the table.

Cixous speaks of inner marginality – of not being at one with self, other, or world – as a kind of living social issue which conditions, but does not determine, existence. She says,

> The dream would be to be there . . . to witness one's own birth . . . my mother the proof, my mother who circulates within me, my mother who is in me as I was in her, what a strange, red, contained link, that doesn't reassemble itself, doesn't stop, that passes, escapes, pursues its course across generations, carrying our colors well beyond ourselves . . . [But] The most surprising is not that I, I will die, it is that I was born, that I am not you, and that I am me. I would like very much to know that me. (Cixous, 1998: 86, 87)

The most surprising thing is not that classroom flexibility is a barrier to full participation of disabled people; nor is it a surprise that accessible washrooms remain closed without notice; nor is the most surprising thing that implementing legislation in order to increase access becomes a justification to not increase access at this time. No, the most surprising thing is that disabled people and disability studies live in the university. It is surprising that disability studies is, for example, tentatively and sporadically beginning from tables built from a need to critically respond to the powers that have ordered life; it is surprising that a time has come where it is possible to reflect on how disabled people, places, and ways of life are produced as less than livable.

That there is any time and place for disability is surprising given bureaucracy's structured necessity to always frame disability in the shape of a 'not-yet,' while excluding disability from conceptions of participation and exempting it from conceptions of 'all.' Moreover, the university is also the primary place that generates masses of individualized, medicalized knowledge of disability which typically represent disability as a kind of deficit or deviance in need of remedy. This is knowledge that feeds the ongoing, historically generated belief that disability acts as a 'natural' disqualifier. Yet, disability lives on in the time and space of university life and work. What Cixous (1998: 87) brings to mind is that from this 'strange, red, contained link, that doesn't reassemble itself,' new things can be born.

People, like traditions, however, cannot witness their own births, even though they can dream them. Instead, we have proof of a past from which, strangely enough, disability studies has emerged – and in regard to which, equally as strange, there is a need to come to know ourselves in relation to how disability studies is taken into account. Proof is everywhere, proof that something, be it mothers, tables, or traditions, came before us and is, in fact, part of what links and forges something new in the here and now. But there is also proof that what has come before is not the whole of disability studies, nor the whole of the meaning of embodiment, nor the whole of what it means to participate from the position of a not-yet participant.

'The most surprising is not that I, I will die, it is that I was born, that I am not you, and that I am me. I would like very much to know that me' (Cixous, 1998: 87). Self-knowledge, by Cixous's account, is steeped in the recognition of difference that has become much more than a marker of death. This difference is born in relation to not being a replica of what gave birth to it. That disability is configured as a not-yet holds many deadly possibilities for all people; in coming to know this while reflecting on being positioned as a not-yet, as partial, and as not at one with what has come before, there may still arise ways of coming to access new questions and thus coming to know the body in social space in new ways.

Cixous's work, then, marks a return of the question of positionality. The sort of positionality that Cixous is characterizing involves self-knowledge; it is a position towards self and other which does not proceed from a belief in the self-evident noticing of difference, since she recommends an exploration of this difference – 'I would like very much to know that me,' she says. Her version of positionality situates inquiry in a not-knowing in the midst of a desire to know. What, who, and where I am now has much to do with trying to get to know what 'proof' lies behind our becoming thus and so.

There is, then, an ethics behind the question of 'when?' Bodies are made sensible over time and in particular places by particular others. Ethics, as Rosalyn Diprose (2005: 238) reminds us, is 'the question of being positioned and taking up a position in relation to others . . . derived from the Greek word *ethos*, meaning dwelling, or habitat – the place to which one returns.' Any way of knowing is related to what is already known. Knowledge of the self, knowledge of critical race theory, feminism, or disability studies, is not to be located *in* these traditions alone. From this more dialogic version of positionality it is but a dream to locate knowledge in the self or in a lone tradition of thought. Instead, knowledge is positioned between us, between the tables that we can and cannot come to; between our bodies at these tables and not at others; between the various symbolic, material ways tables bring us together and how they separate us in relation to various devaluations and disqualifications, such as racism and sexism, against which we continue to labour. Thus, the position of being regarded as a not-yet cannot be fully encapsulated by a negation since this position exceeds its own dismissal by reflecting on this positionality.

It is this 'between space' that is an essential matter to consider if people are going to begin to wonder about how we are made to matter to each other. 'The dream,' says Cixous (1998: 87), 'would be to be there . . . to witness one's own birth.' To believe we can capture complete knowledge of our own origin and possess it in absolute certainty is to pursue a rejection of mysterious conditions of fleshy mortality. Left as a dream, there remains at least the metaphor of 'my mother the proof' – there are all sorts of proofs that I am not the origin of my own making, and that disability studies is not the origin of its existence – but there are new relations to what has come before that are not yet, and hopefully never will be, fully at one with their own genesis.

To not be, as the saying goes, 'a self-made man' is to recognize the promise in the proof that social space and body meet not just as replication, not only as resemblance, and as something more than an effect. The meeting of social space and body represents a potential newness – a constrained creativity, an agentive subjection. In the meeting between social space and embodiment there lies the power of imagination, expressed in the metaphor of 'my-mother-the-proof.' 'Mother' is a metaphor for carrying our colours, conventions, and normativities well beyond ourselves. We could do it, emote it, live it, or be at the table a little differently. We could think about tables and chairs as we leave and enter classrooms; we could imagine a new life arising from the position that holds that bodies are not destiny, as this gives rise to a sense that we are still destined to live through our bodies. To believe that dreams should be left as dreams, and thus not pursue the illusion of complete access to the history of one's own birth, is to live with the proof – that is, a desired mediation of our makings that can question this mediation. Such proof is very different from, or even opposed to, knowledge of our origin. We may have originally intended a wheeled flexibility, but flexibility has been carried well beyond itself. Disability studies may have been invited to the table to add a more nuanced account of oppressive forms of marginalization, only to find that the table itself is changing in shape and even changing the sort of knowledge that will be made there. Still, to seek proof is to come to learn something of that which grounds the possibility of our existence in the lives and stories that we already have become.

The most surprising thing is that disability studies enters the university as that which can turn the tables and claim that disability is not-yet, and hopefully not ever, merely an object of knowledge. The ambiguity of disability studies means that we need to forgo many forms of certainty, and even the certainty of what is believed to be knowable, sayable, doable, and reasonable. Ironically, the work of critical theoretical approaches, such as disability studies, is not generated solely by what it fights (patriarchy, racism, capitalism, able-ism); what links us can also be explored in generation, renewal, genesis, and natality. Being positioned as a not-yet – as not fully at one with any meaning ascribed to us and not fully at one with any of the already legitimized positions of knowledge production – can be a place for the possibility of something new. We should like to get to know this, too, this link to something new, as much as we know the deadly exclusions.

The generative processes before us, those which circulate in us, are where we also circulate, right down to the tables at which we find ourselves – all this has something to do with the kind of subjects we can be as well as the kinds of conversations we can and cannot have. Considering the body in social space as the question of 'when?' gives rise to the possibility of forging new histories, insofar as we can question what has already been made of embodiment. The conversation of disability studies, together with what has helped to bring it to the table, means that people are narrating how they stand, sit, and lie in the spaces between us, at the tables made and arranged not necessarily by our own design – but made nonetheless. The possibility of something new is made by an openness to a politics of wonder that can orient to what has already made us a space of questions. In the next and final chapter, I turn to an exploration of how the questions of who, what, where, and when are differently asked and differently answered when guided by a commitment to a politics of wonder.

6 Towards a Politics of Wonder in Disability Studies

Throughout this book, I have referred to the concept of wonder as potentially a kind of politics.[1] But wonder is political only insofar as embodiment is an interpretive relation between self and world. What is required is that we attend to our interpretations of disability and, in so doing, pay attention to the politics we make use of to respond to the place of disability in our society. Such attention is what I am calling 'wonder,' since to engage with our interpretations is – like interpretation itself – a political act. Wonder, then, is the political engagement with our own politics regarding disability. In this final chapter, I further pursue this politics of wonder. I introduce a conception of the shape and meaning of wonder as a politics which can inform inquiry in order to move towards a fuller exploration of the three final interwoven aims of *The Question of Access*.

The first of these three aims is to discuss the political necessity for social inquiry to resist being dominated by the demands of the question of 'why?' I explore the possibilities and limits of asking 'why?' as a way to invite a consideration of an alternative question, the question of 'how?' Through a discussion of the difference between these two forms of questioning, I show that the question 'how?' can allow for social inquiry that does something other than *explain* what already is and thus resists securing certainty in the status quo.

The second aim is to focus on what the emerging field of disability studies is making of disability within university environments. I will briefly examine how disability studies imagines and questions disability and show how this is both related to and different from the established ways that disability has been an object for university work and life. I do this by examining how disability studies publicly describes

itself in its program descriptions and through calls for disability studies conference papers. Addressing how disability has been interpreted
within disability studies is to politically engage with the act of interpreting disability.

The first two aims are oriented to achieving my final aim, namely, to
demonstrate the primacy of a reflexive form of inquiry that can engage
its own politics and reflexively engage its act of interpreting disability.
These three aims are a way to approach the emerging field of disability
studies through a politics of wonder by treating disability studies as
itself a representation of the relations between bodies and social space,
amenable to theorizing. The pursuit of these three aims culminates in
an exploration of the ways in which asking the who, what, where, and
when questions can lead us away from the common desire to only explain and manage disability by keeping it as an open question. I move
now to a depiction of wonder as grounding an inquiry that might con-
tribute to reflexive politics of embodied life.

Politics of Wonder

'A politics of wonder' is not code for a map or model of disability studies. Instead, I am attempting to find ways to respond to the political
necessity of pursuing a form of disability studies inquiry that can do
something other than produce more of the same. The production of
the same kinds of answers to the questions of 'who, what, where, and
when?' in disability research can lead to a diminished, unimaginative,
and devalued life for disabled people.

The political necessity of pursuing something other than more of the
same is also tied to the following understanding: what if, as Foucault
(1980) claims, it is true that most of what we know and much of what
we can come to know is tied into the reproduction of what-already-is?
In the face of the idea that knowledge reproduces the powers that be,
and that such powers form what is recognized as knowledge, some different way of knowing is necessary. Rosalyn Diprose (2002: 126) puts
it this way: '. . . it is in the generation of new ideas that thinking is
productive in its political task of transforming both the self and the
social realm.' This possibility, suggests Diprose (2002: 128), is tied to
'recasting problems in new and interesting ways.' I understand such a
'recasting' to include a return to reflect on how 'problems' have already
been cast, or what I have called earlier the need for a restless reflexive
return to the way people are already situated.

Recasting requires us to wonder about how things, people, and events have already *cast* their problems. It requires, then, that we address traditional answers to the questions of who, what, where, and when as they relate to disabled peoples' participation in collective life. Wondering is generated through such a recasting, which is a way to start to discern if there might not be some better, more lively and imaginative ways to conceive of a collective's version of problems as well as its versions of answers or solutions.

Regarding the need to wonder, Aimé Césaire (1972: 16, 17) says that the 'domain of the marvelous' is where a kind of knowledge that moves 'beyond the world's crises' can be generated. This is a 'poetic knowledge . . . born in the great silence of scientific knowledge.' If the marvelous and the wondrous are kindred domains, then the politics of wonder within disability studies is a move to return to what is already working to release understandings of the status quo and generate the marvel of new possibilities. While disability is undoubtedly a problem within the sciences, including the social sciences, how this problem of disability has been made obviously beyond question remains quiet in the great silence of science. Asking how problems come to make an appearance, for whom, where, and when, recasts the problem of disability by dislodging it from its taken-for-granted embodied moorings. If the social significance of disability-as-problem can no longer be cast as a strict matter of the body, it is then possible to wonder about how disability as problem comes to appear at the intersection of the perceiver and the perceived (Titchkosky and Aubrecht, 2009). Disability, understood as emerging in the intersection of the perceiver and the perceived, is a space where poetic knowledge also emerges. Poetic knowledge recasts scientific knowledge as the question of how we make the meaning of people, and how we develop our interrelatedness in social space.

And yet the suggestion of 'wonder' and 'politics' working together leads to a host of tricky questions. For example, what is political about wonder? How is theorizing the meaning of what is already said and done by disability studies going to 'do' anything politically significant to the current power relations that dominate what disability means and govern its form of life? What procedural demands accompany the need for disability studies to be open to an inquiry that is based in wonder? It may even seem that there is little hope to be found in the act of wonder when what we face is the oppression of the ruling orders of the day – colonialism, patriarchy, classism, and able-ism, all of which are served and supported by the capitalist enterprise of scientific knowledge production. While it is easy to be dissuaded from locating a politics in the affective activity of wonder, I turn now to a further exploration of a few ways wonder is connected to theorizing and politics.

Wonder as Political Action

It is commonly held that Western *philosophy* begins in wonder and attempts to nurture a sense of wonder. The same, however, cannot be said of the relation between *politics* and wonder. It is not commonly held that productive political paths can be forged through the act of encountering *what is*, reflecting on it, and wondering as to its constitution and meaning. Politics is, instead, more associated with activities oriented towards building future processes and systems while working for or against present material and ideological certainties. Indeed, contemporary conceptions of 'politics' are steeped in a bureaucratized notion of the management of human life where, for example, governance occurs through studied relations to populations and their control. Such a version of politics finds no interest in a connection to the affective activity of wonder and the uncertainty that can accompany it.

A politics of wonder is not an endeavour that works from certainty, nor is it so much about action plans or planning for the control of others' actions. Instead, a politics of wonder arises from the activity of making uncertainty out of what is certain. It is an attempt to engage current political organization, forms of social activity, and structures as spaces of questions. Engaging what already 'is' as a space of questions is a way to practise a form of theorizing that is oriented to something other than explaining life – or, as Charles Lemert (2002: 387) puts it, it is 'to make a story that tells a story that already exists.' Such an orientation permits us to ask *how*; how is it that we find ourselves in the spaces we occupy today and how does our location in a history of activities manufacture where we find ourselves and its meaningfulness? Instead of wonder, however, we typically take for granted the nature of what appears. For example, populations such as 'the disabled,' 'the elderly,' and 'youth' appear as problems requiring study and management that typically generate a myriad of 'why?' questions. What is the extent of the problem and what can be done to resolve it? Why do these populations not respond positively to remedial plans or programs? Such questions represent a bureaucratic governance of peoples' lives. But these problem populations can also represent a place to wonder about the making and the meaning of people and the social scenes we inhabit.

A politics of wonder releases us from the contemporary demand to always serve the primacy of the goal of certainty. This release is not the same as believing that wonder extricates inquiry from power, nor that it transforms the inquirer into a transcendental, contemplative being. Wonder brings us into proximity with certainty but it does not put us at one with certainty. Disability is certainly a problem, and is daily made manifest as such, but its constitution as problem is brought close, paradoxically, by making its certainty questionable. Sara Ahmed (2006: 82–3) suggests,

> To wonder is to remember the forgetting and to see the repetition of form as the 'taking form' of the familiar. It is hard to know why it is that we can be 'shocked' by what passes by us as familiar.

The shock of understanding certainty *as* a question, whether that certainty is the familiar being made strange or the strange being made familiar, permits us to encounter what 'is' as the grounds of and for questioning. How has perception been grounded such that it certainly can and will 'see' the problem that is disability? Still, the possibility of wonder remains in a remembering, a repetition, or a recasting of what has come before in order for it to now appear as a shocking instance of the need to ask 'how?' How is *what-is* possible? This is not disruption for the sake of disruption (debunking) but a disruption for the sake of the possibility of forging new lives together.

In disability studies, questions can be generated by attending to that which grounds the possibility of what has been done to, said, and thought about embodiment. Through re-presenting these grounds in activities which re-enter disability studies – its knowledge production, organization, activism, and arts – a politics of wonder can be realized. The problem of disability can be recast and brought close to people in new ways, moving us to question *how* 'what is' is; for whom, where, and when? Wonder, then, is a political act, a form of questioning oriented to the open-ended need to understand.

Understanding, Hannah Arendt (1994: 308) reminds us, is an 'unending process,' a 'uniquely human way of being alive,' since it is in seeking understanding that new stories are made. The promise of new ways to narrate who people are in relation to each other in the places and times that we find ourselves is undoubtedly a political act since this comes with different ways of being with and for others. Understanding the meaning of disability as it comes to appear in the face of questions of access, of questions of bodies and social space, is a way to pursue the promise that comes with a politics of wonder. With a politics of wonder, we are brought to questions such as 'how do I know disability to be a problem and how does this conception of what is a problem organize my perception of disability?'

The Question of 'How'?

'Why?' is ordinarily the master of all the other W5 questions, and so the 'who, what, where, and when' questions are typically asked in service of the ultimate end – an answer to the question 'why?' The power to say why what is *is*, to assume all things have a knowable cause or a controllable origin, is a contemporary way to secure predictive prowess in human affairs (however mythical this security may be). Asking 'why?' is a legacy of the Enlightenment, with its belief in progress, releasing the power of cause-and-effect rationality that gives rise to explanations that seem to permit people to know, control, and manipulate *what is*.

Such a rationality, however, also produces a version of the world and its people. A belief in a progressive time oriented strictly to the question of 'why?' has potently produced disability only as a problem. Further, disability has become a contemporary scene for the unquestioned assertion of 'why?' currently fostered by the biomedical disciplines. This is a way of knowing that leads easily into providing the sort of information necessary for cost-benefit accounting procedures endemic to contemporary forms of governance, social and health services, as well as personal improvement projects and, ultimately, the naturalization of human devaluation. This is the typical way disability is 'thingified' in the academy today and becomes contained as nothing but an object for research (Crawford, 1980). For example, universities around the globe are engaged in research regarding failing minds, failing learners, failing limbs, the inability to walk, to heal, to sense, to think; the discipline of education researches the workings of 'behaviourals,' their core deficits and learning difficulties, mindblindness, special needs, or confused articulations, and so on and so forth. The way to include and contain the body within the university is a problem which shapes embodiment by the 'why?' question that contains, manages, delineates, and treats it through various knowledge regimes. Disability is made sensible as an object for those legitimate subjects who are today's researchers and knowledge producers. The disabled body understood, unquestionably, as a problem has become so normalized that it serves today as one of the primary cogs in the funding engine for university research on disability.[2]

A politics of wonder, however, is certain that any production of disability as problem is also worthy of examination.

Bodies do show up in the shape of other questions. For example, consider Irving Zola's (1982: 244) question – how has a society 'been created and perpetuated which has excluded so many of its members'? But this alternative form of questioning requires that we orient to asking how disability has come to be understood as a problem in the first place. Until we begin to approach this assumption of the problem of disability with wonder and begin to study *how* it is that these bodies, minds, or senses have been made sense of as problems, the relations between embodiment and the spaces within which we find ourselves are likely to remain the same. Disability, too, is likely to remain a partial participant whose removal from the movements of life is an ever-present possibility.

Recognizing that we are caught in chains of interpretation provides for other stories (Merleau-Ponty, 1958; Smith, 1999a: 98), even about what appears to be unequivocal answers to the question of 'why?' That any answer to why, any articulation of certainty, can be re-framed so as to reveal its interpretive relations makes way for other stories. Attending to the fact that we are not at one with what has grounded our certainties makes it possible to recognize the powers of neo-liberalism's ongoing, medicalized, bureaucratic containment of life as itself a story. This means that certainty can be read as a *metaphorical* expression of life – a metaphorical expression of the socio-political relations that can be forged with what is said, done, thought, and imagined.

Metaphor

Paul Ricoeur (1978: 134) characterizes metaphor as the main problem of meaning making and as the main problem of the *study* of meaning making – hermeneutics itself. Metaphor is the main question of concern; it makes something happen with words by reaching out and forging unexpected connections that open gaps between the ordinariness of things say-able and the extraordinary – namely, new meaning. Metaphor works with what is already known and tries to say how something is like something else, and in so doing shows *how* things, events, and people mean. Of metaphor's significance, Ricoeur (1978: 147) goes on to say that metaphor . . . is related to the function of poetry as a creative imitation of reality . . . for the sake of poiesis [creation] in the mimesis [imitation] . . . If it is true that the poem creates a world, it requires a language which preserves and expresses its creative power in specific contexts.

We pull away from the question of why for the sake of attending to meaning making, and 'for the sake of poiesis in the mimesis.' To make something new from what we already know, think, or say is to ask how what is *is* for us. It is to make a paradox out of what is already made, or what Ricoeur calls a mimesis moving towards poiesis, something I have been calling a politics of wonder. Imitating reality by saying how something means or by showing its grounds of possibility attempts to express the real as a metaphorical meaning. Metaphor is, thus, part of the creation of the world even as it participates in its creation. Making something of what has already been made is again a way to refer to a politics of wonder, or – in Césaire's terms – the poetics of the marvelous.

Bringing his discussion of metaphor to an end, Ricoeur (1978: 148) says:

Allow me to conclude in a way which would be consistent with a theory of interpretation which lays the stress on 'opening up a world.' Our conclusion should also 'open up' some new vistas. On what? Maybe on the old problem of imagination, which I cautiously put aside. We are prepared to inquire into the power of imagination, no longer as the faculty of deriving 'images' from sensory experiences, but as the capacity to let new worlds build our self-understanding . . .

Opening up new vistas requires something other than the assuredness of an inquiry guided by the why question. Developing the capacity to let new worlds build our self-understanding requires an engagement with the already do-able, say-able, and sense-able that lies between self and other, bound in ongoing interpretive chains. This form of engagement that opens up new self-understandings and simultaneously new worlds is captivated by the wonder of the worlds of meaning that we not only inhabit, but that we also are. In an interview discussing her poetic and philosophical texts, Hélène Cixous (2008: 81) characterizes such an approach:

For me, theory does not come before, to inspire, it does not precede, does not dictate, but rather it is a consequence of my text . . . it has been to respond to a moment of tension in cultural current events, where the ambient state of discourse – academic discourse, for example, or journalistic or political discourse – has pushed me to go back over things, to stop my journey and take the time to emphasize . . . So all that is called, 'theoretical' in my work is in reality simply a kind of halt in the movement . . .

A politics of wonder, too, 'goes back over things'; it goes back over what already is as it metaphorically expresses what people, times, and places must already mean to and for one another; what Cixous describes as that which has been possible to read for a long time.

What is possible to read, since at least the time of the Enlightenment, is that some people are 'problem-things' in need of management and redress. In our reading of this, Cixous recommends that we 'halt,' or develop a politics that will allow us to wonder and thus create new relations to that which we find in the space of our halting. This is not an application of theory to the world. Instead, Cixous suggests that this halt is itself a kind of theoretic approach that can reveal who people are in the places where, over time, we come to be metaphorically mediated meanings of life for each other, yet to be understood. In the midst of the certainty of appearing to and for one another as problems, we can halt and re-enter this with a politics of wonder that renders it uncertain – and that provides for what Ricoeur calls a poiesis in mimesis, telling a story of the stories we've already told.

The Who, What, Where, and When of Disability Studies

With this understanding of a politics of wonder, I turn to analysis of certain disability studies' self-descriptions. Attending to the ways in which disability studies describes itself will give us a taste of the play of metaphor as well as the kinds of worlds that disability studies is opening. Such self-descriptions can remind us about what is so easily forgotten in the contemporary approach to embodiment as always a problem-thing in need of explanations. Here is a random selection of disability studies' self-descriptions that was found on the Internet.

Disability studies is[3]
. . . finding acceptance as a university discipline
. . . a small, dynamic, hands-on program
. . . growing rapidly
. . . a new discipline, emerging only in the last few decades

. . . still an emerging discipline, but is changing the landscape of the academy from the ground up
. . . marginalized within academia
. . . the perfect place for committed, passionate people who want to help enhance the well-being of all
. . . essentially an activist endeavour
. . . a way to improve rehabilitation and community services
. . . interdisciplinary, grounded in liberal arts, particularly a humanities approach
. . . not about learning about different types of impairments
. . . changing people's perspective about what it is and how to affect change
. . . arising from the activities of the disabled people's movement and following the 'social model of disability'
. . . interdisciplinary because it draws upon the intellectual tools of the major disciplines and because it serves as a conceptual framework that reorients the basic assumptions of various fields of knowledge, from political science to architecture, from . . .
. . . mainly a graduate field of study
. . . broaden[ing] our race, class, and gender discussions to include layers of identity and moments of connection
. . . among the hippest and newest fields in American academia
. . . hot!
. . . located within the Faculty of Health Sciences
. . . exploding in the humanities disciplines
. . . a sub-field of the social sciences
. . . a national agenda
. . . an emerging area of great potential
. . . still seeking to define itself
. . . at the cutting edge of the widening academic study of disability
. . . largely overlooked
. . . both timely and relevant
. . . a professionally oriented program
. . . available to teachers in lesson plans and various teaching resources
. . . now accepting applications

Whatever else disability studies is, its metaphoric representations occur in the midst of a host of competing, even contradictory, meanings of what it is to be/do disability studies today. Interestingly enough, this selection of descriptions has nothing to say about *why* disability studies is. Even if we were to 'read between the lines' and claim that disability studies is arising at this time because of the social model of disability or activism – or because of the growing interdisciplinary impulse within the university milieu – or because of a need to bring the body back in, these causes would not override the sense in which the meaning of disability studies is situated in a jumble of differing relations to embodiment. Treating disability studies as caused by contradictory impulses would not mean understanding this emerging field.

In the midst of these contradictory meanings of disability studies, there are meanings of disability that do emerge; for example, disability is not represented as simply a problem. None of the different expressions have anything to say about disability as inability, lack, dysfunction, or absence – the 'disability' of disability studies is not impairment based. The version of disability that is metaphorically expressed by these descriptions is more like a somewhere, a something, articulated at a particular historical time for others to take interest in as *something other than* a problem. The question remains, though, how is disability being made to mean and how is it being represented in these descriptions?

Let's halt at this remarkable fact that in these disability studies descriptions – bodies-as-functions, impairments, physical, sensory, emotional, or intellectual matters seem almost to be missing. In this absence, disability studies' interest in disability certainly differs from all the disciplines that have come before. But it would be absurd to think this is merely a new way to avoid the topic of embodiment; disability studies has found something to study and is today producing a variety of research and artistic works, not to mention self-descriptions, all which have something to do with embodiment. Insofar as little mention is made of what Rod Michalko (2002) calls 'bodies gone wrong,' the body-of-interest for disability studies lies elsewhere. The body-of-interest that disability studies attends to is located in the social processes through which embodiment is conceived of and thematized by people. What disability studies 'is' is a discipline interested in embodiment as it is shaped by the interests of others. Disability for disability studies is, then, an always-already-mediated phenomenon, and thus no attempt is made to provide a (mythical) unmediated mention of the body in the disability studies self-descriptions.

The certainty that the body is a problem thing, upon which so many disciplines have based their work, is revealed to be ambiguous by disability studies as it expresses itself without referring to embodiment as such a thing. Disability studies demonstrates that there is no body that is not interlaced with the interests of its perceiver. The certainty of the problem becomes, ironically, the ambiguity which is necessary for disability studies to wonder about how disability has been thematized as a problem for and by others. Metaphoric mediation is thus crucial to understanding the meaning of disability for disability studies, as well as to continue to wonder a little more about its everyday self-expressions.

Given that disability studies' self-descriptions mediate disability's meanings, the activities of the actual words used are also there to consider. Whether disability studies is bursting on the scene or slowly emerging; whether it is established or a hot new interdisciplinary adventure gaining a hold within current disciplines, it is nonetheless depicted as socially, politically, and historically located. This holds true whether disability studies is articulated as marginal within the academic scene, as an enterprise that rejects typical approaches to the study of disability, or as something that comes to the aid of those who do treat bodies, minds, and senses as problems in need of solutions. Disability studies can be described in all these seemingly contradictory ways insofar as 'disability' is being located among dominant knowledge producers. It is this locale of representation that disability studies finds itself in and to which it attends.

The various self-descriptions by disability studies perform relations to embodiment as a socially located phenomenon. Described as a field that is slowly growing, emerging, new, bursting on the scene, it demonstrates a relation to disability that is historical. Considered as a part of the humanities, social sciences, health studies, liberal arts, or as interdisciplinary, all such descriptions have something to say about disability studies' academic location. This diverse located-ness attests to disability studies' tacit understanding that disability does not hold a singular meaning. Disability studies, then, can be read for its revelation of the plurality *that is disability*. Disability studies' self-descriptions, taken together, suggest that it might appeal to graduate students, activists, professionals, and the academy, and this demonstrates that an interest in disability arises in community with others. Within the list of possible things to be said about disability studies today we are, yet again, given access to disability as a set of relations to questions regarding what, where, when, and who.

Recall Paul Ricoeur's (1974: 134; 1981: 181) work on metaphor where 'imagination is treated as a dimension of language.' Disability as a metaphor for ambiguous certainty makes disability a prime place to consider the phenomenon of imagination. Disability studies is a space of imagination, but not because disability is an image or object derived from sensory experience. Even when faced with scientific stances that seek to separate, as much as is possible, the subjective act of noticing from the noticed object, disability studies does not proceed in the ways that other disciplines do. Instead, it imagines disability as a form of perception tacitly made use of by those disciplines that imagine disability to be a concrete object of study. Disability studies thematizes how disability has been noticed by others and treats this noticing as a metaphoric expression of our relations to embodiment.

Noticing how others have noticed (studied) disability requires us to know disability as an imaginative scene where we might build our self-understanding. Disability is an imaginative scene built from how other disciplines, other times, and other people already identify and understand disability. Charles Taylor suggests that the identification of what we can notice, as well as the identification of who we are, is woven with the threads of our inter-relatedness. So, all identity, and subsequent self-understanding, finds its sense in the

> interchange of speakers. I define who I am by defining where I speak from, in the family tree, in social space, in the geography of social statuses and functions, in my intimate relations to the ones I love, and also crucially in the space of moral and spiritual orientation within which my most important defining relations are lived out. (Taylor, 1989: 33)

What is this community of speakers that is disability studies? Where does it, they, we, speak from? What sense of a family tree might be supporting, feeding, blocking, or otherwise participating in this interchange of speakers?

A key site of interchange for disability studies is those enterprises that attempt to study embodiment as a self-evident problem. In the midst of the 'interchange of speakers' where disability studies speaks, there are also those who speak of disability as an asocial, apolitical, and ahistorical object for study. Disability studies is tied to an exchange with those articulations of disability as the problem body where disability is taken as an (unessential) condition that people must overcome, adjust to, or succumb to. The family tree of disability studies is that space of cultural contradiction where the meaning of humanity is questioned and remade in the midst of other disciplines and activities that continue to deny disability any connection to the question of being human. This raises the question of disability studies' intimacies such that it is compelled to speak to those that regard disability as an abnormal biological condition.

In the interchange of speakers that includes, as Taylor says, intimate relations with the ones we love, disability studies comes to represent an alternative relation to what is loved within contemporary Western(ized) societies – namely, the certain and unambiguous sense of the body achieved through science. Disability studies emerges as a way of being engaged, but not fully at one, with the individualization of disability as a personal tragedy. It is engaged but not at one with the ongoing medicalization of bodies, minds, senses, emotions. Disability studies is also engaged but not at one with the disciplining of disability as a problem for which individuals must seek cure and care, adjustment and adaptation. Finally, disability studies demonstrates an intimacy with the sense that disability is more, other, different, or not at one with whatever disability is already said and known to be. Thus, the notion that disability is interesting only as a problem is itself a problem for those called to the disability studies table (Abberley, 1998). Or, as Bill Hughes (2007: 673) puts it, 'almost by definition, [we] assume disability to be ontologically problematic, and many disabled people feel that many of the people with whom they interact in everyday situations treat them as if they are invisible, repulsive or "not all there."'

Disability studies is a way of recasting the problem of disability; it works in relation to those speakers that are always potentially present participants in casting the problem of disability as an individual and medical one. Such articulations are part of the family tree and demonstrate an intimate love/hate relationship. Through an incantation of resistance, disability studies is engaged with these others. Those who objectify disability are eerie family members against which disability studies cultivates its identification, its response, and its aim to make a difference by providing something more than an objectified version of disability.

A most common disability studies practice, however, is to notice and to say what disability studies *is not*. This need for a sense of what we are not and what we do not do is a repetitive practice in the field. Disability is in tension with non-disability, and disability studies is in tension with what is not disability studies – and there is still more. Between the terms of engagement that make up the family tree there is more going on than disability and disability studies being 'not that!' I now engage this *not that*.

Not That!

Disability studies' reiteration and habitual evocation of 'we are not that!' appears not only in the self-descriptions above, but also in articles, books, presentations, programs, and policy. Through the invocation of 'not that!' a connection to what we do not wish to be becomes part of what disability studies is remaking and representing. This self-definition achieved through the evocation of what-I-am-not is, as Taylor suggests, a crucial space of moral and spiritual orientation within which our most important defining relations are lived out. Claiming 'we are not that!' expresses an 'us/them' or 'insider/outsider' dichotomy (Bauman, 2000), and this creates a disability-studies-identity through an articulation of difference. But could this recognition of a divisive dichotomy be too quick, too easy, too satisfying? What does this familial habit of thought and practice have to say about disability studies today?

There is a need to remember what has been forgotten in the creation of any us/them dichotomy (Ahmed, 2006: 82–3). Consider comments such as: 'They are medicalizing disability,' or 'That is just another way to individualize disability,' or even 'Like everyone else, they too treat disability as nothing but a problem' . . . and, of course, 'We're not that!' Note the familiarity of the endless repetition of the family tree with those who we say are 'not us,' even as we forever leave chairs around the table of disability studies for 'them' to occupy. The resistance of the individualization and medicalization of disability as a problem serves to establish disability studies' identity in relation to that which it and we resist.

According to phenomenologist F.G. Asenjo (1988), revealing the meaning of people, places, or things is to reveal the interrelatedness of the terms used to refer to them. Asenjo (1988: 23) says that 'a relation is not only a chain like connection but also the actual medium in which terms originate.' In the chains between self and other, disability studies and non-disability studies, problem and solution, there is the actual medium within which these terms originate. This medium is the act of recognition, or what Taylor refers to as the family tree; the nexus of statuses and identifications to which we are related and in relation to which we speak. Out of the terms that provide for the possibility of identification of disability studies, we have the chains of relations to which disability studies is tied.

The terms by which we refer to others are the 'condensations of ambiguous' changing relations which serve as the 'medium that envelops perception itself' (Asenjo, 1988: 24, 28). Along with the chains of difference, where people in disability studies claim that 'we are not that,' there is also the provision of the terms that mediate the perception of identity and difference in the first place. As a way to explore some terms that envelop the perception of disability studies, I turn to a 2008 call for papers for the first annual graduate student disability studies conference in Canada, which was held at York University. The terms of the call were put this way: 'Critical Disability Studies Student Association invites submissions from any discipline . . . as long as they pertain to a disability-related theme.' This call addressed through a politics of wonder leads to the question: 'What is on the interdisciplinary table of disability studies?'

The call invites work on 'a disability-related theme,' any theme, which means that we can perceive disability as a theme taken as a form of relatedness. The call invites us to understand disability as a thematic of life – and there are various ways disability can theme-our-life, since there are a variety of ways that we relate to disability. Regarding disability as a 'theme' means not perceiving disability as a thing in a linear march that reproduces the problem/solution discourse. As a theme, disability is mediated as, for example, stigma, oppression, exclusion, policy issue, or activist struggle, or as a way to take interest in ways we currently can take interest in the world. To address disability as a theme is to have the opportunity to perceive disability as more complicated than a personal tragedy of a medical nature which restricts an individual's ability to accomplish tasks of daily living in a way considered normal. It is more complicated, since understanding disability as theme requires that we examine what it means to propose that disability represents personal tragedy, medical substance, and/or restrictions of individual activities addressed and remedied by experts. The implications of this is that disability studies is 'more than' the repetitive act of noticing that disability studies is 'not that.'

The interpretive chain of relations that disability studies examines – for example, the individualization of disability through science – is the medium of perception that disability studies also needs to examine as it nurtures its own sense of self. The medium of not-doing what individualizing does, for example, grounds what disability studies can say about itself. A recognition of disability studies and its others is accomplished in relation to the terms of who, what, where, and when disability studies does its work. The terms of engagement of disability studies, those familial terms, are also the medium of its perception.

Recognition and the Question of Access[4]

Disability studies aims to resist the individualization of embodiment and, in so doing, calls upon the terms of individualization as well as the disciplines or discourses actively involved in that process. The terms of the process of individualization chain disability studies to a particular set of relations. But these terms are also the origin of the perception of disability as a social matter. The dichotomy between those who individualize disability and those who perceive it as a social – and not an individual – phenomenon is not really an either/or situation, nor is the significance of this dichotomy adequately recognized if we regard it as collapsible into one another (or avoid it altogether). The dichotomy needs to be recognized as a space of mediation, that is, as a space of questions, since it 'is' part of the act of recognizing what lies between us.

Us/them, social/individual, disability studies/not disability studies – these are not merely dichotomies. They are mediums of interaction; terms of reference set in contexts not necessarily of our own choosing, such as classroom design teams that speak of wheelchair users as a 'worst-case scenario,' large university buildings with misleading access signs, or missing accessible washrooms that are not noticed as missing. It is true that in justifying the absence of accessible features in the university environment, disability is individualized in every case. But recognizing only this would be to miss how the individualization of disability is the medium of perception for asking a host of questions, such as who belongs, where, and when? The terms of reference that mediate our relatedness are how we wonder about space and begin to develop questions regarding it. What is provocative is the sort of questions that can and cannot arise as these are mediated by the imaginative relations to the places where we find ourselves, and live and work as embodied beings.

That recognition appears in the midst of the daily difficulties of living together is what *The Question of Access* calls attention to. The stories of how we are coming to recognize access as a problem are also the terms of recognition that bring to consciousness the actual practices that mediate what belonging might look like. Crucially, this entails turning to the everyday terms that are used in the act of noticing and struggling for access. Recognition and non-recognition of a lack of access are social actions intimately engaged in the practice of making up the meaning of people. Turning to practices of daily life so as to attend to the routine act of noticing people, places, things, events, and bodies as questions of access is to locate inquiry in the midst of our relatedness. Such noticing is achieved through the medium of recognition; the medium of our making.

But herein lies a difficulty – how are we to want to attend to this productive process of everyday life when it seems as though 'recognition' is a simple act which is good when present and terrible when not? In fights for access, for example, it seems that access is either recognized as a problem or it is not, or that people either have access or do not. Embedded in either/or thinking, it is difficult to regard all these either/or forms of recognition as the actual terms from which the perception of access can arise as a question, and through which its meaning is forged. When present/not present becomes the only question, it submerges a consideration of the actual productive workings of recognition – and thus a consideration of how access is already a form of perception from which springs the 'doing' of what it means to live together, whether physical access changes or not. Practices of recognition are constitutive of the meaning of our living together, so what are we doing when we recognize each other in this way or that through the question of access? How might we not let this question drop away?

Many-Sided Recognition

In her essay, 'Eye to Eye,' Audre Lorde (1984) tells many stories that can be read as raising the issue of recognition. From her adult perspective, she writes of being seen as a child on the streets of her city neighbourhood, in the bus, at the library, and in the doctor's office. She narrates the act of being recognized as a 'black girl' in these ordinary daily scenes of life; she is recognized through contempt, downcast eyes, leers, and eyes of hate. In her recounting of those 'looks,' the reader is positioned to better understand what it means to know that any relation of recognition – including hate – is simultaneously the medium of our making. Through these face-to-face, or 'eye-to-eye,' encounters, Lorde recounts how she was made to experience herself as a devalued other.

Lorde turns to these moments to undertake an act of recognition of her own. She tells us of a desire to take into account the anger of being forced to incorporate a response to others' destructive recognition of her into her self-understanding. In wondering about how others perceive her, Lorde rereads and rewrites how she was inscribed as the devalued other. Part of this act of recognition includes a narrative of likely one of Lorde's first memories of her movement towards legal blindness. Of this move, accomplished through yet another derogatory face-to-face encounter, Lorde says:

> My three-year-old eyes ache from the machinery used to test them. My forehead is sore. I have been poked and prodded in the eyes and stared into all morning. I huddle into the tall metal and leather chair, frightened and miserable and wanting my mother. On the other side of the eye clinic's examining room, a group of young white men in white coats discuss my peculiar eyes. Only one voice remains in my memory. 'From the looks of her she's probably simple, too.' They all laugh. One of them comes over to me, enunciating slowly and carefully, 'OK, girly, go wait outside now.' He pats me on the cheek. I am grateful for the absence of harshness. (Lorde, 1984: 148)

Peculiar eyes, probably simple, certainly black – these moments of recognition make a mere absence of harshness into a welcome gesture. From her adult position, recognizing these moments of her sore flesh and emotions, Lorde lifts this towards her reader so as to achieve a different sort of recognition. Through her 'eye to eye' story, we come to perceive the limiting ways a racist scopic regime makes belonging and worth appear and disappear. The slow spoken words of 'OK, girly, go wait outside now' touch us as patronizing, able-ist racism for which she was, at the time, 'grateful.' Eye to eye – through white eyes, the look of her skin combined with a look at her eyes led into a moment of recognition that made for a radical disqualification – 'From the looks of her she's probably simple, too.' Simple, feeble-minded, beneath contempt. Simple (like 'crazy') – a form of recognition that functions as a mechanism to strip people of their human rights and their legal status, and even strip people of their basic status as human altogether. Still, Lorde's words represent a recognition. She recognizes the reader's need to grapple with the social fact that any relation of recognition is also the medium through which the term 'human' is made and unmade. This brings us to the threshold of the medium of recognition through which the meanings of people are produced – and this is no small wonder!

The life that is recognized as no-life is often found at the nexus of race and disability. This nexus is found marking those recognized as disqualified. Saying this, however, is very different from saying that racialized people are disabled by racist and patriarchal society. Neither is this reference to the nexus of disability and race a prosthetic moment where disability is used to prop up race as a social issue and vice versa. Rather, through Lorde's narrative, we can notice that the terms of our identification combine to make moments of recognition into the meaning of human/non-human life itself. To argue whether one term of recognition trumps another as a form of disqualification – or to argue that all these terms are the same – is to miss the necessity of turning critical theoretic consideration onto *the actual use of the terms of recognition*, and onto our key concepts and metaphors. These terms are put to use as productive processes through which life and death; pleasure, pain, and relief; and human and non-human are made.

Acts of recognition, including those that belong to questions of access, mark the difficulty of regarding recognition as a practice, and thus as a form of oriented and productive social action. Words of recognition are the acts of narrating what we are. Lorde's eyes are recognized by herself as peculiar, as something of interest to others, to be brought to eye clinics, to be poked and prodded, to be delivered a miserable unfamiliarity. They are eyes that become signs of further troubles, such as interactions with white men in white coats who leave behind bad memories of 'OK, girly, go wait outside now'; they become food for thought in an essay called 'Eye to Eye' – in all this lies the complex process of recognition. This is the many-sidedness of recognition. Recounted by Lorde, recognition brings us face-to-face with the wondrous complexity of perception, of which and to which we are all subject in many different ways.

The many-sidedness of recognition resides in the complexity of and between every word. Words provide access to worlds. Words are the mediation of the relations between us and are able to remake these worlds. This is perhaps what Asenjo (1988: 24) meant when he said, 'Words, then, must be taken as ephemeral condensations of ambiguous malleable relations; they are the local incarnation of global meanings, meanings which vary in the process of writing, reading, re-writing, and re-reading.' 'Access' is just such a word; a word that actualizes a relation of recognition through which the meaning of who, what, where, and when is made and remade. All of this ambiguity can be transformed into the conventional practice of recognition that takes shape as certainty – 'I know her!' or 'I know the problem!' This reductionist version of recognition gives us Audre Lorde as a set term in the chain of North American existence; a marginalized person who managed to access her inclusion in history. For example:

> . . . born in New York City to Caribbean immigrants Frederick Byron Lorde and Linda Gertrude Belmar Lorde, who settled in Harlem. Nearsighted to the point of being legally blind, and the youngest of three daughters, Lorde grew up hearing her mother's stories about the West Indies. She learned to talk while she learned to read, at the age of four, and her mother taught her to write at around the same time. She wrote her first poem when she was in eighth grade. (http://en.wikipedia.org/wiki/Audre_ Lorde, accessed March 16, 2008)

Adequate recognition? Fundamental inclusion? If this is access, what have we been given access to? Is being recognized as objectively present presence enough? Again, we are provoked to ask, When we get in, what are we in for? Recognition is too much when it is too little and makes us too little when it becomes too much.

The Need for a Politics of Wonder

The first task in generating a politics of wonder in relation to the social act of recognition is to perceive recognition as something other than a measurable quantity – and as other than the have/have-not form of discernment so common to neo-liberal orientation. We can move towards some relation to recognition that does something other than participate in a 'scopic regime' (de Certeau, 1984: 91) that enforces versions of each other from above, a distancing-look mapping out the certainty of types (race, class, gender, sexuality, location, and sometimes . . . disability). We need to get in touch, from below, with how we appear to and for each other. Disability is not merely a word to be added into the chain of our existence; it is not the et cetera clause of identity politics. Instead, disability and questions of access are normatively ordered, ongoing forms of recognition and communication accomplished between people.

Still, we need to recognize and wonder about a scopic regime that measures the presence and absence of accessibility as though this is unrelated to the mediation of human meaning and social space. It is necessary to establish a relation to recognition that reflects and theorizes its own practices and can question what it means to act and perceive as we do. This is *to move between* the terms that mediate our existence and do something other than set up chains of known relations, one trumping the other. Thus who has access, and to what? What space do we occupy and how? What does it mean to not only experience access or its absence but also to come to notice ourselves and others through questions of access?

The fight for access gives us the recognition that access is a form of perception that can permit us to wonder about the politics that generate our relations to embodiment. The fight for the value of differential embodiment gives us access to the world from which such a fight arises. Connecting the terms disability and access constructs, potentially destroys, and certainly mediates the meanings of human life (Butler, 2009: 33). For these reasons, *The Question of Access* must always remain a space for questioning. The terms through which we already recognize each other provide access to the possibility of wondering about constituted relations between bodies and social space. Engaging the terms and interests of fights for access invites us to wonder about belonging. Who are we when we belong, and where? This is the politics of wonder.

Notes

Preface

1 The social model of disability (Oliver, 1990, 1996) suggests using 'disabled people' rather than the more popular phrase 'people with disabilities.' People-first language or separating people from both their embodied differences and the social environment (as the government of Canada and WHO recommend) has not significantly changed the oppressive everyday meaning of disability. For discussion, see Michalko, 2002; Overboe, 1999; Pothier and Devlin, 2005; Titchkosky, 2001a, 2007a.

1. Introduction

1 Access is an abiding research, legal, educational, and policy issue in disability studies literature; for a little taste of this research area, consult Barnes and Oliver, 1995; Barton, 2006; Barton, Barnes, and Oliver, 2002; Mace, 2008; Charlton, 2003; Chouinard, 2001; Disability Archive at University of Leeds, 2007; Disability World, 2006; Frazee, 2005; Kumari Campbell, 2010; Pothier and Devlin, 2003; Livingston, 2000; McColl and Jongbloed, 2005; Opini, 2006; Prince, 2009, 2004a, 2004b; Rioux, 2002; Schweik, 2009; Stienstra, 2006; Titchkosky, 2006, 2003b, 2000; Tremain, 2005.
2 See note 1 in the preface of this volume.
3 My interpretive sociological approach to disability studies is informed by phenomenology and hermeneutics.
4 First presented as 'Disability Culture and Community Development,' keynote address for the 3rd Annual Breaking Down Barriers Conference of Canada-Wide Accessibility for Post-Secondary Students, Toronto, December 2006.

5 For the variety of ways that literacy is a taken-for-granted problem, see Brown and McGreevy, 1994; Gunning, 2006; for ways it is theorized, see Meek, 1992; Peters, 2005; Slee, 2008; Titchkosky, 2008b, 2007a, 2005; Winzer, 2005.

6 Recognizing that the other perceives disability as a version of failed human-ity, and asserting that we are 'not that,' may not adequately address that this version of humanity itself is in need of critical reflection. See page 143 in this volume.

2. 'Who?': Disability Identity and the Question of Belonging

1 Both the concept 'BIU' (basic income unit) and critiques for this way of imagining students are present throughout Western(ized) academia. Some literature does more than point out that the transformation of education into a commodity makes students both consumer and consumed. For ex-ample, Kevin Love (2008) conceives of education as the process whereby people are 'put in question.' By this, Love means the sort of questioning that ' troubles totality . . . enjoys no closure . . . in such a way as to then re-instigate the question' (27). The ongoing commodification of education is thus critiqued for its inability to support such questioning.

3. 'What?': Representing Disability

1 A version of this chapter was first presented at the 'Unruly Salon,' University of British Columbia, 2007. Another version is published as Titchkosky, 2009.

2 Corker, Conrad, Fanon, Foucault, Michalko, Murphy, Razack, Stiker, Thomas, Wendell, and Zola are a few examples of authors that can be read as sharing a common commitment to theorizing how disability is pointed at as a scientific, bureaucratic-legal, and common-sense problem. On theoriz-ing the act of pointing, consult Dorothy Smith, 'Telling the Truth after Post-modernism' (1999a).

3 Understood as their condition, disabled people *have* been made to dis-appear; e.g., disabled people have been the object of both soft and hard eugenic programs (Russell, 1998; Snyder and Mitchell, 2006b; Titchkosky, 2005).

4 Disability studies artists, scholars, and/or activists.

5 Since the writing of this book, this situation has changed, for example, new signs of a similar design are now found near accessible doorways.

4. 'Where?': To Pee or Not to Pee

1 This chapter was first presented at the 7th Annual Second City Conference on Disability Studies in Education (Chicago, 2007) and a version of this is published as Titchkosky, 2008a, ' "To Pee or Not to Pee?" ' A special thanks to Len Barton whose engaged discussion with me undoubtedly enhanced my analysis.

2 For further consideration of the governance of embodiment/disability and imagination, see, for example, Ahmed, 2006; Bhabha, 1994; Butler, 1997; Diprose, 2005; Frazee, 2005; Foucault, 1988; Goodley, 2010, 2007; Lindgren, 2004; Michalko, 2002; Parekh, 2006; Shildrick and Price, 1996; Stiker, 1999; Thomas, 2004; Tremain, 2005.

3 An amalgam of narratives is related to Peter Clough's (2002: 8) suggestion that bringing together various narrative fragments that arise in a given locale is a method that protects the anonymity of the speakers while allowing the theorist to 'speak to the heart of consciousness.' Acknowledging Canadian tri-council ethical concerns, my narratives harm no one since no individual is represented and the narratives stem from my daily round of life where no collection of narratives was embarked on (see van den Hoonaard, 2000; Canadian Institutes of Health Research, 2005; Gubrium and Holstein, 2002). What are represented in these narratives are things that are say-able and treated by all involved as sensible (Campbell, 2003; Gadamer, 1996, 1991; Sacks, 1984; Scott, 1998, 1995; Smith, 1999b, 1990; van Manen, 1990).

4 For empirical documentation regarding exclusion, consider the Canadian government's own representations of it (HRDC, 2006; Canada, 2004; or Prince, 2009; McColl and Jongbloed, 2005), which shows the combined unemployment, underemployment, and non-labour force participation rate for 'persons with disabilities' to be around 80 per cent. The United Nations (2003–04) has characterized the fate of disabled people around the globe as a 'silent crisis.' For the severity of the exclusion and marginalization of disabled people, please consult Barnes, 1998; Charlton, 2003; Dossa, 2009; Erevelles, 2000; Jones, 1994; Oliver, 1996, 1990; Rioux, 2002.

5 Mairtin Mac an Ghaill (2000: 314) says that '[a]n idealist analysis of the curriculum that reduces the heterosexist structuring of schooling to aberrant teacher prejudice is insufficient to explain the complex social interaction of white male and female teachers with black male students in racialized, male dominated institutions.' I follow through on this understanding as it connects with other physical and ideological educational structures. In this way, I avoid the need to say that really it is strong or weak curriculum, or

really it is good or bad physical structures that lead to the radical devaluation of disability in the Canadian educational milieu. Instead, having been
made by culture, disability – in relation to textbooks *or* washrooms – is a
good place to examine culture.

6 Canadian government counts of the population of 'people with disabilities' have varied between 3.6 and 4.2 million people; the majority of those
counted are of working age (15–65) and the majority of these people are said
to have a mild or moderate mobility or agility impairment (HRDC, 2006;
Canada, *Advancing 2004*, especially appendix A). For other disability rates,
see www.disabilityworld.org/links/Research, accessed November 15, 2007.

7 Unlike these four washrooms, the final 'accessible' washroom bears no sign
of gender, can be found on the uppermost floor, and was made more accessible in 2007. Still, this washroom also does not meet minimum university
accessibility standards.

5. 'When? Not Yet': The Absent Presence of Disability

1 For more traditional historical accounts of the university, consider Ford,
1985; Friedland, 2002; Lang and Eastman, 2001.

2 First presented to the Canadian Disability Studies Association meetings of
the Congress, Ottawa, 2009, and the 22nd Annual International Society for
Disability Studies Conference, Tucson, AZ, 2009; see also Titchkosky, 2010.

3 As a further illustration of the need to rethink 'all,' consider that in a
2010 CAO Memo ('Accessibility Closure Notification,' March 3, 2010) all
students, faculty, and staff were informed: 'Under the Accessibility for
Ontarians with Disabilities Act (AODA) – Customer Service Standard organizations are required to provide notification regarding the unavailability
of facilities that are normally relied upon by persons *with mobility impairment* in accessing services or activities within our buildings. These include
substantive disruption or closure of elevators, access ramps, accessible
parking stalls, barrier-free washrooms and key auto-opening access doors.
The University and OISE have created signage that will be placed at or near
any of the above facilities should there be an extended period of service
disruption . . . It is recommended that persons with permanent or temporary *mobility impairment* check . . . web-site on a regular basis to ensure that
facilities that they depend upon are not closed due to any service disruption' (emphasis added). 'All' has been transformed by this notification into
people with 'mobility impairments' and demonstrates the essential need to
rethink collective taken-for-granted relations to disability in order to remake
the history of exclusion.

4 First delivered as a public lecture, 'Our Bodies in Social Space: Developing the Conversation between Disability Studies and Feminism,' for the Centre for Women's Studies in Education, OISE/UT, Toronto, February 5, 2009.
5 For a more, extensive discussion of between-ness as it relates to the doing of disability studies, please see my 'Betwixt and Between: Disability is No-Thing,' in *Disability, Self and Society* (Titchkosky, 2003a).
6 For more, consult Steven Drakes, Blog from *Not Dead Yet* (July 17, 2009), 'Peter Singer in the NY Times: Disabled Lives Worth Less, Hypothetically,' http://networkedblogs.com/p7559928, accessed February 12, 2011.

6. Towards a Politics of Wonder in Disability Studies

1 This chapter was first presented as a keynote address, 'The God Trick in Disability Surveys: The Need for a Politics of Wonder in Disability Studies,' at the Critical Disability Studies Graduate Conference, York University, May 2, 2008.
2 On this point, consider the following news item: 'Report Estimates U.S. Health Research Funding at $122 Billion. In a troubling repeat of last year, the U.S. investment in research to improve health remains flat at 5.5% of all health-related spending. Research! America's recently released 2007 *Investment in U.S. Health Research* report estimates that the amount spent on research increased from $116 billion in 2006 to $122 billion in 2007 . . .,' www.researchamerica.org/advocate_jan09#investment, accessed February 21, 2011.
3 Thanks to Anne E. McGuire for compiling this list from available Internet websites in North America in 2009.
4 First presented as a keynote address, 'Recognizing Disability and Race and All that Lays Between,' at the SESE 11th Annual Graduate Student Conference, 'The Fecundity of Recognition: The Self/Other in Politics, Sociality, Ethics, and Critique,' April 4, 2009.

References

AODA. (2005). *Accessibility for Ontarians with Disabilities Act* (Accessibility Standards for Customer Service, Ontario Regulation 429/07, AODA: 13). http://www.mcss.gov.on.ca/NR/rdonlyres/FEE69AC5-45FA-4DDF-88FD-F6309550C3C8/4645/GuidetotheAccessibilityStandardsforCustomerService.doc, accessed February 12, 2011.

Abberley, Paul. (1998). The spectre at the feast: Disabled people and social theory. In T. Shakespeare (Ed.), *The disability reader: Social science perspectives* (pp. 79–93). London: Cassell Academic.

Agamben, Giorgio. (2005). *State of exception.* Kevin Attell (Trans.). Chicago: University of Chicago Press.

Ahmed, Sara. (2006). *Queer phenomenology: Orientations, objects, others.* Durham, NC: Duke University Press.

– (2007). 'You end up doing the document rather than doing the doing': Diversity, race, equality and the politics of documentation. *Ethnic and Racial Studies, 30*(4), 590–609.

Arendt, Hannah. (1958). *The human condition.* Chicago: University of Chicago Press.

– (1973). *On the origins of totalitarianism.* New York: Harcourt Brace Jovanovich.

– (1994). *Arendt: Essays in understanding: 1930–1954.* New York: Harcourt Brace and Company.

Asenjo, F.G. (1988). *In-between: An essay on categories.* Lanham, MD: Center for Advanced Research in Phenomenology and the University Press of America.

Barnes, Colin. (1998). The social model of disability: A sociological phenomenon ignored by sociologists? In T. Shakespeare (Ed.), *The disability reader: Social science perspectives* (pp. 65–78). London: Cassell Academic.

Barnes, Colin & Mike Oliver. (1995). Disability rights: Rhetoric and reality in the UK. *Disability & Society, 10*(1), 111–16.

Barton, Len (Ed.). (2006). *Overcoming disabling barriers: 18 years of disability and society.* London: Routledge.

Barton, Len, Colin Barnes, & Mike Oliver (Eds.). (1997). *Disability studies: Past, present and future.* Leeds: The Disability Press.

– (2002). *Disability studies today.* Cambridge: Polity Press.

Bauman, Zygmunt. (1990). *Thinking sociologically.* Oxford: Blackwell.

– (2000). *Liquid modernity.* Malden, MA: Blackwell Publishing.

– (2004). *Identity.* Malden, MA: Polity Press.

Berger, Peter. (1963). *Invitation to sociology: A humanistic perspective.* New York: Anchor.

Bhabha, Homi K. (1994). *The location of culture.* New York: Routledge Classic.

Brown, Sandra & William McGreevy. (1994). *Experiencing reading.* Dubaque, IA: Kendall/Hunt Publishing.

Butler, Judith. (1993). *Bodies that matter: On the discursive limits of sex.* New York: Routledge.

– (1997). *The psychic life of power.* Stanford, CA: Stanford University Press.

– (2009). *Frames of war: When is life grievable?* New York: Verso Press.

Campbell, Marie. (2003). Dorothy Smith and knowing the world we live in. *Journal of Sociology & Social Welfare, 30*(1), 3–22.

Canada. (2002). *A profile of disability in Canada, 2001 tables: 2001 participation and activity limitation survey.* Ottawa: Housing, Family and Social Statistics Division.

– (2004). *Advancing the inclusion for people with disabilities 2004: A government of Canada report: Executive summary.* Ottawa: Office for Disability Issues.

Canadian Institutes of Health Research, Natural Sciences and Engineering Research Council of Canada & Social Sciences and Humanities Research Council of Canada. (2005). *Tri-Council policy statement: Ethical conduct for research involving humans.* Ottawa: Public Works and Government Services Canada.

Césaire, Aimé. (1972). *Discourse on colonialism.* New York: Monthly Review Press.

Charlton, James I. (2003). Challenging geographies of ableness: Celebrating how far we've come and what's left to be done. *Canadian Geographer, 47*(4), 383–5.

Chouinard, Vera. (2001). Legal peripheries: Struggles over disabled Canadians' places in law, society and space. *Canadian Geographer, 45*(1), 187–92.

Cixous, Hélène. (1998). *Stigmata: Escaping texts.* New York: Routledge.

– (2008). *White ink: Interviews on sex, text and politics.* New York: Columbia University Press.

Cixous, Hélène & Jacques Derrida. (2001). *Veils.* Stanford, CA: Stanford University Press.

Clare, Eli. (2002). Flirting with you. In *Gendered bodies: Feminist perspectives.* http://www.disabilityhistory.org/dwa/queer/paper_clare.html, accessed July 14, 2008.

Classen, Constance. (1993). *World of sense: Exploring the senses in history and across cultures.* London: Routledge.

Clough, Peter. (2002). *Narratives and fictions in educational research.* Buckingham, UK: Open University Press.

Cohen, Jeffrey Jerome, & Gail Weiss (Eds.). (2003). *Thinking the limits of the body.* New York: State University of New York Press.

Corker, Mairian. (2001). Sensing disability. *Hypatia, 16*(4), 34–52.

Crawford, Robert. (1980). Healthism and the medicalization of everyday life. *Journal of Health Sciences, 10*(3), 365–88.

Darke, Paul. (1998). Understanding cinematic representations of disability. In T. Shakespeare (Ed.) *The disability reader: Social science perspectives* (pp. 181–200). London: Cassel Academic.

Davis, Lennard J. (1995). *Enforcing normalcy: Disability, deafness and the body.* London: Verso Press.

– (2006a). The end of identity politics and the beginning of dismodernism. In Lennard J. Davis (Ed.), *The disability studies reader*(2nd ed.) (pp. 231–42). New York: Routledge.

– (Ed.). (2006b). *The disability studies reader* (2nd ed.). New York: Routledge.

De Certeau, Michel. (1984). *The practice of everyday life.* Berkeley: University of California Press.

Diprose, Rosalyn. (2002). *Corporeal generosity: On giving with Nietzsche, Merleau-Ponty, and Levinas.* New York: State University of New York Press.

– (2005). A 'genethics' that makes sense: Take two. In M. Shildrick & R. Mykitiuk (Eds.), *Ethics of the body: Postconventional challenges* (pp. 237–58). Cambridge, MA: MIT Press.

Disability Archive at University of Leeds. (2007). http://www.disability-archive.leeds.ac.uk, accessed November 15, 2007.

Disability World. (2006). Disability World Links: Research. http://www.disabilityworld.org/links/Research, accessed November 15, 2007.

Dossa, Parin. (2006). Disability, marginality and the nation-state – Negotiating social markers of difference: Fahimeh's story. *Disability & Society, 21*(4), 345–58.

– (2009). *Racialized bodies, disabling worlds: Storied lives of immigrant Muslim women.* Toronto: University of Toronto Press.

Dowd, Maureen. (2005, September 3). United States of shame: Stuff happens. *The New York Times:* Opinions. http://www.nytimes.com/2005/09/03/opinion/03dowd.html, accessed September 3, 2005.

Dyer, Richard. (1993). *The matter of images: Essays on representations.* London: Routledge.

Erevelles, Nirmala. (2000). Educating unruly bodies: Critical pedagogy, disability studies, and the politics of schooling. *Educational Theory, 50*(1), 25–47.

Farley, Anthony Paul. (1997). The black body as fetish object. *Oregon Law Review, 76,* 457–535.

Featherstone, Mike, Nigel Thrift, & John Urry. (2005). *Automobilities.* Thousand Oaks, CA: Sage.

Ferguson, Susan & Tanya Titchkosky. (2008). The contested space of the body in the academy. In Anne Wagner, Sandra Acker, & Kimine Mayuzumi (Eds.), *Whose university is it, anyway?* (pp. 61–76). Toronto: Sumach Press.

Ferri, Beth & David Connor. (2006). *Reading resistance: Discourses of exclusion in desegregation and inclusion debates.* New York: Peter Lang.

Finkelstein, Vic. (1998). Emancipating disability studies. In T. Shakespeare (Ed.), *The disability reader* (pp. 28–49). London: Cassel Academic.

Ford, Anne Rochon. (1985). *A path not strewn with roses: One hundred years of women at the University of Toronto.* Toronto: University of Toronto Press.

Foucault, Michel. (1978). *The history of sexuality: Volume I: An introduction.* New York: Vintage Books.

– (1980). *Power/knowledge: Selected interviews and other writings 1972–1977.* New York: Pantheon Books.

– (1988). Technologies of the self. In Luther H. Martin, Huck Gutman, & Patrick H. Hutton (Eds.), *Technologies of the self: A seminar with Michel Foucault* (pp. 16–49). Amherst: University of Massachusetts Press.

Frazee, Catherine. (2005). Exile from the china shop: Cultural injunction and disability policy. In M. McColl & L. Jongbloed (Eds.), *Disability and social policy in Canada* (2nd ed.) (pp. 357–69). Toronto: Captus Press.

Friedland, Martin. (2002). *The University of Toronto: A history.* Toronto: University of Toronto Press.

Gabel, Susan L. (Ed.). (2005). *Disability studies in education: Readings in theory and method.* New York: Peter Lang.

Gadamer, Hans-Georg. (1991). The conflict of interpretations: Debate with Hans-Georg Gadamer. In M.J. Valde (Ed.), *A Ricoeur reader: Reflection and imagination* (pp. 216–41). Toronto: University of Toronto Press.

– (1996). *The enigma of health: The art of healing in a scientific age.* Jason Gaiger & Nicholas Walker (Trans.). Stanford, CA: Stanford University Press.

Garland-Thomson, Rosemarie. (1997). *Extraordinary bodies: Figuring physical disability in American culture and literature.* New York: Columbia University Press.

Gilroy, Paul. (2000). *Against race: Imagining political culture beyond the color line.* Cambridge, MA: Harvard University Press.

Goffman, Erving. (1963). *Stigma: Notes on the management of a spoiled identity.* New York: Penguin Books.

Goodley, Dan. (2007). Towards socially just pedagogies: Deleuzoguattarian critical disability studies. *International Journal of Inclusive Education, 11*(3), 317–34.

– (2010). *Disability Studies: An interdisciplinary introduction.* London: Sage.

Graduate Student Association. (2008). Accessibility Committee, *Mandate,* Ontario Institute for Studies in Education of the University of Toronto. http://www.oise.utoronto.ca/gsa/Accessibility_Committee.html, accessed February 12, 2011.

Graham, Linda & Roger Slee. (2008). Inclusion? In Susan Gabel & Scot Danforth (Eds.), *Disability and the politics of education: An international reader* (pp. 81–99). New York: Peter Lang.

Grosz, Elizabeth. (2003). Histories of the present and future: Feminism, power, bodies. In Jeffrey Jerome Cohen & Gail Weiss (Eds.), *Thinking the limits of the body* (pp. 25–38). New York: State University of New York Press.

Gubrium, Jaber F. & James A. Holstein (Eds.). (2002). *Handbook of interview research: Context and method.* Thousand Oaks, CA: Sage.

Gunning, Thomas G. (2006). *Assessing and correcting reading and writing difficulties* (3rd ed.). Boston: Pearson Education.

Heap, James. (1991). A situated perspective on what counts as reading. In Carolyn D. Baker & Allan Luke (Eds.), *Towards a critical sociology of reading pedagogy: Papers of the XII world congress on reading* (pp. 103–29). Amsterdam: John Benjamins Publishing.

Howes, David. (1991). *The varieties of sensory experience: A sourcebook in the anthropology of the senses.* Toronto: University of Toronto Press.

Hughes, B. (2007). Being disabled: Towards a critical social ontology for disability studies, *Disability & Society, 22*(7), 673–84.

Hughes, Bill & Kevin Paterson. (1997). The social model of disability and the disappearing body: Towards a sociology of impairment. *Disability & Society, 12*(3), 325–40.

Human Resources Development Canada (HRDC). (2006). *Advancing the Inclusion of Persons with Disabilities.* http://www.hrsdc.gc.ca/en/hip/odi/documents/advancingInclusion06/toc.shtml, accessed November 15, 2007.

Hunt, Paul. (1998). A critical condition. In T. Shakespeare (Ed.), *The disability reader: Social science perspectives* (pp. 7–19). London: Cassell Academic.

Ingstad, Benedicte & Susan Reynolds Whyte (Eds.). (1995). *Disability and culture*. Berkeley: University of California Press.

Jenkins, Richard. (1998). Culture, classification and (In)competence. In Richard Jenkins (Ed.), *Questions of competence: Culture, classification and intellectual disability* (pp. 1–24). Cambridge: Cambridge University Press.

Jones, Ruth J.E. (1994). *Their rightful place: Society and disability*. Toronto: Canadian Academy of the Arts.

Keohane, Kieran & Carmen Kuhling. (2004). *Collision culture: Transformations in everyday life in Ireland*. Dublin: The Liffey Press.

King, Thomas. (2003). *The truth about stories: A native narrative*. Toronto: Dead Dog Café Inc. and CBC.

Kumari Campbell, Fiona. (2010). *Contours of ableism: The production of disability and abledness*. Basingstoke, UK: Palgrave Macmillan.

Lang, Daniel & Julia Eastman. (2001). *Mergers in higher education: Lessons from theory and practice*. Toronto: University of Toronto Press.

Lemert, Charles C. (2002). Poetry and public life. *Cultural Studies/Critical Methodologies, 2*(3), 371–91.

Levinas, Emmanuel. (1996). Martin Heidegger and ontology. *Diacritics, 16*(1), 11–32.

Lindgren, Kristin. (2004). Bodies in trouble: Identity, embodiment, and disability. In Bonnie G. Smith & Beth Hutchinson (Eds.), *Gendering disability* (pp. 145–65). New Brunswick, NJ: Rutgers University Press.

Livingston, Kathy. (2000). When architecture disables: Teaching undergraduates to perceive ableism in the built environment. *Teaching Sociology, 28*(3), 181–91.

Lorde, Audre. (1984). *Sister outsider: Essays and speeches*. Freedom, CA: Crossing Press.

Love, Kevin. (2008). Higher education, pedagogy and the 'customerization' of teaching and learning. *Journal of Philosophy of Education, 42*(1), 15–34.

Mac an Ghaill, Mairtin. (2000). (In)visibility: 'Race,' sexuality, and masculinity in the school context. In J. Iseke-Barnes & N.N. Wane (Eds.), *Equity in schools and society* (pp. 313–30). Toronto: Canadian Scholars' Press.

Mace, Ron. (2008). Universal design. http://www.design.ncsu.edu/cud/about_ud/about_ud.htm, accessed December, 2008.

McColl, Mary Ann & Lyn Jongbloed (Eds.). (2005). *Disability and social policy in Canada* (2nd ed.). Toronto: Captus Press.

McGuire, Anne & Rod Michalko. (2011). Minds between us: Autism, mindblindness and the uncertainty of communication. *Journal of Educational Philosophy and Theory, 43*(2), 162–77.

McHugh, Peter. (1968). *Defining the situation: The organization of meaning in social interaction.* Indianapolis: Bobbs-Merrill Company.

McRuer, Robert. (2006). We were never identified: Feminism, queer theory, and a disabled world. *Radical History Review, 94*(Winter), 148–54.

Meek, Margaret. (1992). *On being literate.* Portsmouth, NH: Heinemann.

Merleau-Ponty, Maurice. (1958). *Phenomenology of perception.* London: Routledge and Kegan Paul.

Michalko, Rod. (1998). *The mystery of the eye and the shadow of blindness.* Toronto: University of Toronto Press.

– (1999). *The two-in-one: Walking with Smokie, walking with blindness.* Philadelphia: Temple University Press.

– (2001). Blindness enters the classroom. *Disability & Society, 16*(3), 349–59.

– (2002). *The difference that disability makes.* Philadelphia: Temple University Press.

– (2010). What's cool about blindness. *Disability Studies Quarterly, 3/4.* http://www.dsq-sds.org/article/view/1296/1332, accessed November 14, 2010.

Michalko, Rod & Tanya Titchkosky. (2001). Putting disability in its place: It's not a joking matter. In Wilson & Lewicki-Wilson (Eds.), *Embodied rhetorics: Disability in language and culture* (pp. 200–28). Carbondale: Southern Illinois University Press.

– (2010). There and not there: Presence and absence of disability in the transition from education to work. In Peter Sawchuck & Alison Taylor (Eds.), *Challenging transitions in learning and work: Reflections on policy and practice* (pp. 109–24). Rotterdam, the Netherlands: Sense Publishers.

OCUFA (Ontario Confederation of University Faculty Associations). (2008). *March 31, 2008. Budget 2008 Ontario's Post-Secondary Spending Plans: OCUFA Working Papers Series.* http://www.ocufa.on.ca/workingpapers/Budget Analysis-OCUFA-2008.pdf, accessed May 2009.

Oliver, Michael. (1990). *The politics of disablement.* Hampshire, UK: MacMillan Press.

– (1996). *Understanding disability: From theory to practice.* New York: St. Martin's Press.

Opini, Bathseba M. (2006). Strengths and limitations of Ontario post-secondary education accessibility plans: A review of one university accessibility plan. *International Journal of Inclusive Education, 12*(2), 127–49.

Overboe, James. (1999). 'Difference in itself': Validating disabled people's lived experience. *Body& Society, 5*(4), 17–29.

Parekh, Pushpa Naidu. (2006). Gender, disability and the postcolonial nexus. *Wag.a.du: A Journal of Transnational Women's and Gender Studies (4).*

http://web.cortland.edu/wagadu/Volume%204/articles4.html, accessed November 15, 2007.

Peters, Susan. (2005). Transforming literacy instruction: Unpacking the pedagogy of privilege. In Susan L. Gabel (Ed.), *Disability studies in education: Readings in theory and method* (pp. 155–72). New York: Peter Lang.

Pothier, Dianne & Richard Devlin (Eds.). (2003). *Critical disability theory: Essays in philosophy, politics, policy, and law.* Vancouver: UBC Press.

Prince, Michael J. (2004a). Canadian disability policy: Still a hit-and-miss affair. *Canadian Journal of Sociology, 29*(1), 59–82.

– (2004b). Disability, disability studies and citizenship: Moving up or off the sociological agenda? *Canadian Journal of Sociology, 29*(3), 459–67.

– (2009). *Absent citizens: Disability politics and policy in Canada.* Toronto: University of Toronto Press.

Razack, Sherene. (2008). *Casting out: The eviction of Muslims from Western law and politics.* Toronto: University of Toronto Press.

– (2010). Abandonment and the dance of race and bureaucracy in spaces of exception. In Sherene Razack, Malinda Smith, & Sunera Thobani (Eds.), *States of race: Critical race feminism for the 21st century.* Toronto: Between the Lines.

Ricoeur, Paul. (1974). *The conflict of interpretations.* New York: Continuum International Publishing Group.

– (1978). *The philosophy of Paul Ricoeur.* Boston: Beacon Press.

– (1981). *Hermeneutics and the human sciences.* John B.Thompson (Ed.). Cambridge: Cambridge University Press.

Rioux, Marcia H. (2002). Disability, citizenship and rights in a changing world. In Colin Barnes, Len Barton, & Mike Oliver (Eds.), *Disability studies today* (pp. 210–27). Cambridge: Polity Press.

Russell, Marta. (1998). *Beyond ramps: Disability at the end of the social contract.* Monroe, ME: Common Courage Press.

Sacks, Harvey. (1984). On doing 'being ordinary.' In J. Maxwell & J. Heritage (Eds.), *Structures of social action: Studies in conversation analysis* (pp. 413–30). Cambridge: Cambridge University Press.

Schutz, Alfred. (1970). *On phenomenology and social relations.* Chicago: University of Chicago Press.

Schweik, Susan. (2009). *The ugly laws: Disability in public.* New York: New York University Press.

Scott, Joan. (1995). Multiculturalism and the politics of identity. In John Rajchman (Ed.), *The identity in question* (pp. 3–20). New York: Routledge.

– (1998). Deconstructing equality-versus-difference: Or the uses of postcolonial structuralist theory for feminism. *Feminist Studies, 14*(1), 32–50.

Sen, Amartya. (2006). *Identity and violence: The illusion of destiny.* New York: Norton.

Shildrick, Margrit & Janet Price. (1996). Breaking the boundaries of the broken body. *Body & Society, 2*(4), 93–113.

Shklar, Judith N. (1990). *The faces of injustice.* New Haven: Yale University Press.

Singer, Peter. (2008). 'Happy nevertheless: Harriet McBryde Johnson.' *New York Times,* December 28: MM34.

Slee, Roger. (2008). 'Beyond special and regular schooling? An inclusive education reform agenda.' *International Studies in Sociology of Education, 18*(2), 99–166.

Smith, Dorothy E. (1990). *The conceptual practices of power: A feminist sociology of knowledge.* Toronto: University of Toronto Press.

– (1995). *Institutional ethnography: A sociology for people.* Lanham, MD: AltaMira Press.

– (1999a). 'Telling the Truth after Postmodernism.' *Writing the social: Critique, theory, and investigations* (pp. 96–129). Toronto: University of Toronto Press.

– (1999b). *Writing the social: Critique, theory, and investigations.* Toronto: University of Toronto Press.

Snyder, Sharon & David Mitchell. (2006a). *Cultural locations of disability.* Chicago: University of Chicago Press.

– (2006b). Eugenics and the racial genome: Politics at the molecular level. *Patterns of Prejudice, 40*(4–5), 399–412.

Statistics Canada. (2006). *Participation and activity limitation survey 2006: Tables.* Ottawa: Ministry of Industry.

Stienstra, Deborah. (2006). The critical space between: Access, inclusion, and standards in information technologies. *Information, Communication, and Society, 9*(3), 335–54.

Stiker, Henri-Jacques. (1999). *The history of disability.* William Sayers (Trans.). Ann Arbor: University of Michigan Press.

Taylor, Charles. (1989). *Sources of the self: The making of the modern identity.* Cambridge, MA: Harvard University Press.

Thomas, Carol. (2004). How is disability understood? An examination of sociological approaches. *Disability & Society, 19*(6), 569–83.

Titchkosky, Tanya. (2000). Disability studies: The old and the new? *Canadian Journal of Sociology and Anthropology, 25*(2), 197–224.

– (2001). Disability: A rose by any other name? – 'People-first' language in Canadian society. *Canadian Review of Sociology and Anthropology, 38*(2), 125–40.

– (2003a). *Disability, self, and society.* Toronto: University of Toronto Press.

– (2003b). Governing embodiment: Technologies of constituting citizens with disabilities. *Canadian Journal of Sociology, 28*(40), 517–42.

– (2005). Disability in the news: A reconsideration of reading. *Disability & Society, 20*(6), 653–66.

– (2006). Policy, disability, reciprocity? In Mary Ann McColl & Lyn Jongbloed (Eds.), *Disability and social policy in Canada* (2nd ed.) (pp. 54–72). Toronto: Captus Press.

– (2007a). *Reading and writing disability differently: The textured life of embodiment.* Toronto: University of Toronto Press.

– (2007b). Ordering choice: Women, disability and medical discourse. In Ed Ksenych & David Liu (Eds.), *The pleasure of inquiry: Readings in sociology* (pp. 323–400). Toronto: Thomson Nelson.

– (2008a). 'To pee or not to pee?' Ordinary talk about extraordinary exclusions in a university environment. *Canadian Journal of Sociology, 33*(1), 37–60. http://ejournals.library.ualberta.ca/index.php/CJS/article/view/1526/1058, accessed February 12, 2011.

– (2008b). 'I got problems with my reading': An emerging literacy. In Susan L. Gabel & Scot Danforth (Eds.), *Disability and the politics of education: An international reader* (pp. 337–52). New York: Peter Lang.

– (2009). Disability images and the art of theorizing normality. In special issue of *International Journal of Qualitative Studies in Education*, Leslie Roman (guest ed.), *22*(1), 75–84.

– (2010). The not-yet-time of disability in the bureaucratization of university life. *Disability Studies Quarterly, 30*(3–4), n.p. http://www.dsq-sds.org/article/view/1295/1331, accessed February 24, 2010.

Titchkosky, Tanya & Katie Aubrecht. (2009).The power of anguish: Remapping mental diversity with an anti-colonial compass. In Arlo Kempf (Ed.), *Breaching the colonial contract: Anti-colonialism in the US and Canada* (pp. 179–99). New York: Springer.

Titchkosky, Tanya & Rod Michalko (Eds.). (2009). *Re-thinking normalcy: A disability studies reader.* Toronto: Canadian Scholars'/Women's Press.

Tremain, Shelley (Ed.). (2005). *Foucault and the government of disability.* Ann Arbor: University of Michigan Press.

United Nations. (2003–4). *Enable: United Nations commitment to advancement of the status of persons with disabilities.* Department of Economic and Social Affairs: Division for Social Policy and Development. http://www.un.org/esa/socdev/enable/disun.htm, accessed November 15, 2007.

University of Toronto. (n.d.). *Memorandum of Agreement between the Governing Council of the University of Toronto and the University of Toronto Faculty Asso-*

ciation. http://www.governingcouncil.utoronto.ca/policies/memoagr.htm, accessed April 1, 2010.

– (2002). Employment Equity Report, 7. Toronto. http://www.hrandequity. utoronto.ca/Assets/reports/ee/2002.pdf?method=1, accessed June 26, 2009.

– (2004). Governing Council Statement of Commitment Regarding Persons with Disabilities, November 1, 2004. http://www.governingcouncil. utoronto.ca/policies/disabled.htm, accessed July 20, 2009.

– (2008). *Employment Equity Report*. http://www.hrandequity.utoronto.ca/ Assets/reports/ee/2008.pdf, accessed March 26, 2010.

UPIAS. (1976). *Fundamental principles of disability*. London: Union of the Physically Impaired Against Segregation.

van den Hoonaard, Will. (2000). Is research-ethics review a moral panic? *Canadian Review of Sociology and Anthropology, 28*(1), 19–37.

van Manen, Max. (1990). *Researching lived experience: Human science for an action sensitive pedagogy*. London, ON: Althouse Press.

Watts, Ivan Eugene & Nirmala Erevelles. (2004). These deadly times: Reconceptualizing school violence by using critical race theory and disability studies. *American Educational Research Journal, 41*(2), 271–99.

Weber, Max. (1947). *The theory of social and economic organization*. New York: The Free Press.

Weiss, Gail. (2003). The body as a narrative horizon. In Jeffrey Jerome Cohen & Gail Weiss (Eds.), *Thinking the limits of the body* (pp. 25–38). New York: State University of New York Press.

Winzer, Margaret. (2005). *Children with exceptionalities in Canadian classrooms*. Toronto: Pearson.

World Health Assembly (WHO). (1980). *International classification of impairments, disabilities and handicap (ICIDH): A manual of classification relating to the consequences of disease*. Published in accordance with resolution WHA 29.35 of the 29th World Health Assembly.

Zola, Irving K. (1977). Healthism and disabling medicalization. In Ivan Illich, Irving Zola, John McKnight, Jonathan Caplan, & Harley Shaiken (Eds.), *Disabling professions* (pp. 41–68). London: Marion Boyars Publishers.

– (1982). *Missing pieces: A chronicle of living with a disability*. Philadelphia: Temple University Press.

Index

workplace environments, and
access, 16, 71; and conceptions of
disability, 93, 109; expectations in,
45, 80; procedures of accessibility,
103–4

wonder, 6, 83; as political
engagement, 129, 133, 150. *See also*
politics of wonder

words, importance of, 148

World Health Organization (WHO),
disability definition, 5, 9, 45–6,
52

'worst case scenario,' disability as,
32, 33, 34, 35, 37, 56, 145

yes/no relation to access, 35–6, 41

Zola, Irving, 25, 135